# THE
# DREAMS
# LIST

# THE DREAMS LIST

Unleash the Extraordinary Power
of Turning Someday into Today

ALEX FUNK

Paperback ISBN: 979-8-89316-154-0
Ebook ISBN: 979-8-89316-155-7
Hardcover ISBN: 979-8-89316-156-4

To Dane Espegard, for teaching me how to dream.

To my parents, for always making me feel supported and for showing us that anything is possible as long as you live generously and treat people the right way.

And to my dream partner, Ana, for living this extraordinary life with me.

# TABLE OF CONTENTS

## SECTION 3: Achieving Your Dreams (How)

# PREFACE
## What is a Dreams List?

**H**ave you ever wondered what it takes to break free from the expectations of others and truly live out your dreams?

In three years, while earning the same average income as a police officer, nurse, entry-level accountant, or concrete worker, I was able to take eighty-six flights, buy two real estate investment properties, run a treadmill marathon, compete in a bodybuilding show, and cross off two hundred fifty-two other dreams... all before I was twenty-three years old. This started during the COVID-19 pandemic of 2020, when I dropped out of college and moved back into my parents' basement in a small town of a thousand people. So, I'd say no one is more surprised than I am about the life I've been creating. But I also take ownership that I have designed all of this, and have created very duplicatable strategies and systems that *don't involve income.*

The catalyst behind this transformation? A Dreams List - similar to the Bucket List we are all familiar with, but more real, more present, and more meaningful. The Dreams List is designed to help you clarify and articulate your aspirations. It's a structured approach to transform your abstract dreams into concrete goals. Think of the Dreams List as your personal roadmap. It guides you in dissecting your goals into actionable tasks, helping you navigate the journey from where you are now to where you want to be, no matter how big or small.

The creation of this book started over three years ago. Ten weeks into training for the marathon, I realized how many lessons I was pulling from the journey. I had never run more than a mile before this and was realizing that the marathon *training* itself was the hardest thing I'd ever done. So, I started journaling the lessons each week. After all was said and done, and I had completed the 26.2 miles on a treadmill by myself (thanks to the COVID lockdown), I had a notebook full of notes, lessons, and ideas.

That notebook was pulled back out three months later on a nine-hour flight to Oahu, a Dreams List destination for the twenty-one-year-old dropout me. By the end of those nine hours, I had turned an autumn of lessons into a clear book outline: *26.2: A Step-by-Step Blueprint to Accomplishing Even Your Wildest Dream.*

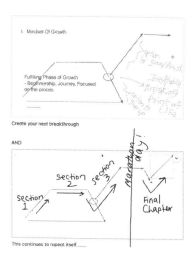

From March until December that year, my goal was to turn that outline into a fully written (very rough) first draft, which I finished on December 29th, exactly one year from the date of my marathon. Upon posting about it on social media and being connected to the publishing company, *Scribe Media*, by the mentor who started all of this dreaming, Dane Espegard, I got a seat at their book publishing workshop the next August in Austin, Texas.

At that workshop, the concept of my book *26.2* was encouraged, but questioned about who would read it, why the story would resonate with anyone else, and if a book like that could create the impact I was hoping for. Leaving the workshop, I had scrapped my one-and-a-half-year project, but had far more clarity about who I was trying to serve with this book and what the message would be, which led to many changes in the subsequent months.

From **26.2: A Step-by-Step Blueprint to Accomplishing Even Your Wildest Dream**

To **Fighting Insignificance: The Eye-Opening Roadmap That I Wish I Had as a Small-Town Kid**

I started re-writing and re-purposing the entire book. Journal page after journal page was filled as I tried to figure out where this book would go. Thanks to another mentor, Mike Monroe, joining the process, we found our passion project.

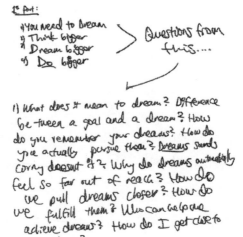

In the end, I opted to write a book to help people realize their deepest dreams and desires, based on human psychology and science, explained through the lens of fascinating historical stories.

*The Dreams List* is divided into three sections.

The first, Lifestyle Design, encourages you to question established norms and redefine your understanding of success and purpose. It quickly debunks the notion of 'I don't have enough money/time.'

The second part introduces the 'Dreams List', a goal-setting and personal development technique that encourages individuals to think big and foster a mindset of limitless possibilities.

The final section provides practical, executable strategies for achieving these dreams, such as time management, energy awareness, habit formation, and recognizing and celebrating accomplishments.

I know that saying, "I live my Dream Life every day," will create jealousy in some people; anger, skepticism, and discomfort in others, but my goal is to inspire and guide a select few who are open to learning how to create the life of **their** dreams. They are who I'm writing this book and creating this mission for.

**Are you one of them?**

# INTRODUCTION
## Escaping the Ordinary Path

## Before the Dreams List

I grew up in a small Minnesota town, where everyone knew (everything about) everyone else.

I can tell you with certainty that I was not born extraordinary. My life should have been fairly *ordinary*.

The middle child, middle cousin. My childhood and teenage nickname was "Gek", short for geek and I dealt with self-esteem and self-confidence issues well past high school. I'm a college dropout.

I was the kid who did whatever it took to be liked, to be seen, to be approved of. Which drove me to become homecoming king, to not quit sports I wanted to quit, and to not try things I wanted to try like musicals and more arts. I was too embarrassed to risk peer scrutiny to be outside the ordinary.

Life was seemingly set for me: graduate, attend college, then probably return to a blue-collar job back home or take over my dad's electrical business.

However, I always knew I wanted to create more for myself than this typical life path.

I had dreams of working for my home state NFL team, the Minnesota Vikings. As a kid, I always had entrepreneurial ideas and ventures, like being the commissioner of fantasy football leagues and selling custom cutting boards out of high school woodshop (until we got *too many* pre-orders and the school district shut it down).

I just never actually thought these things were possible in the real world. Traveling, fancy cars, and big houses all seemed otherworldly, only happening in the movies. I couldn't see that world for myself.

## The Turning Points

Then, during my senior year of high school at the state hockey tournament, I met a guy who actually worked for the Vikings. I told him of my *dream*. He had also given a TED talk, had lunch with the state governor, and done more things that seemed impossible to me with my small-town beliefs.

A few months later, he reached out and told me if I wanted it, he had a job lined up for me with the team working home game days. This was the turning point. It was the first time I was exposed to a world where my dreams could be a reality and it happened so fast; right place right time. Thank you, Michael Sullivan. I remember crying on the way home from interviewing at the Vikings headquarters. It was all so surreal to me, having my own wildest dream come true.

At this same time, I started dabbling in day trading, enticed by the promise of getting rich and inspired by the hope of getting to live my dreams. This led me to quickly losing all of my money.

It wasn't until the same friend who introduced me to the stock market also introduced me to the world of sales, that I was able to start building a career that would give me everything I was looking for. Of all the sales jobs, it was slinging kitchen cutlery where I learned the world of sales and entrepreneurship. Shoutout, CUTCO and everyone at the factory in Olean, NY.

This moment came at a perfect time, as COVID-19 hit soon after and forced me out of my college bubble, which later served as a blessing in disguise.

## The Transformation

I then took a few leaps of faith and never looked back.

I left college for good, immediately invested $10k into a life coach and mentorship community, and dove fully into personal development.

By the way, I didn't even have the $10k, but I knew this was the type of education I wanted. So I used student loan money. Obviously, I don't advise anyone to do this. It's a personal choice and risk I was willing to take at the time, and it worked for me. My goal with this book is to teach you how to do all of this without a big financial investment upfront; maybe ever. I lived in my parents' basement, listened to tens of thousands of minutes of podcasts, read dozens of self-help and business books, and started chasing down dreams on my "Dreams List."

That COVID year, I trained for a marathon, moved to the big city, and really started a new life.

I was no longer the kid seeking approval; I was a man chasing his dreams.

## Success and New Perspectives

Today, I am a completely different person from the Alex of even three short years ago who started writing the treadmill marathon book.

I earned the title of the 'fastest rising star' in a $300m sales organization in my first few years and early twenties, managing multiple record-breaking or top producing offices.

I currently own four real estate units that could let me retire from "working" if I really wanted to.

On top of the marathon, I've done a bodybuilding show, trained to become a boxer (this one didn't last too long), and am now working on being in the best shape of my life, for the rest of my life, through sustainable lifestyle and food choices with aspirations of becoming an American Ninja Warrior.

I'm an author, a podcast guest, and a life and sales coach to many.

I've crossed off hundreds of big and small dreams, including:

◈ Climb a mountain

◈ Buy a property with my parents

◈ Never feel like I'm working a day in my life

◈ Get to 16 inch biceps

◈ Call my mom once a week

◈ Thank a soldier and shake their hand

◈ Get verified on social media (even if I paid for it)

◈ Go to the NFL draft every year

◈ Touch lava (counting solidified basaltic lava in Maui)

◈ See the changing of the guard live

(and 400+ others that you can find at the back of the book - a dreams stealing opportunity for you.)

## Then and Now: Money Mindsets

It hasn't all been easy. Through this journey of leveling up, I have battled with my relationship with money more than anything.

Once, I thought money was evil, and that wealth meant taking advantage of others.

I felt guilty for my success. So guilty that I was embarrassed at times to go home and be around my old friends and family. I just *knew* they thought that I thought I was better than them. Some of them even said as much. It took a while for me to realize that their issue with my success was just that, *their* issue. I shouldn't feel guilty for wanting more or pursuing my passions.

Now, I see money as a tool for bettering my life and the lives of others. I give generously, and I'm transparent about my financial success. I'm trying to bring people with me.

Money, I've learned, is a game of strategy and understanding. Just like mastering a video game, board game, or anything else that requires knowledge and skill, you have to know your enemy to defeat it.

The funny thing is, now that I've fixed my mindset, money is no longer the enemy.

## Lessons Learned

My mindset shift didn't happen overnight. It involved stepping out of my comfort zone, changing my environment, and surrounding myself with people who uplifted me.

It's about understanding that taking control of your finances and daily habits are the keys to living the life of your dreams, not earning more.

**What truly changed everything for me was being ready to take control.**

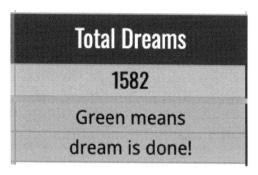

Now it's your turn.

# Lifestyle Design (Why Dream?)

# CHAPTER 1
# We Don't Live to Survive Anymore

To fully understand how we got here, we first have to understand how we all started. Let's take a journey back to an era when survival of the fittest was not just the name of the game but the only way to advance the human race.

Picture a time when dense forests echoed with the roars of predators, and every rustle of leaves signaled potential danger. Nights were lit only by the flickering light of campfires, and our ancestors walked through this challenging terrain on foot. They had to rely on their basic instincts and sharp senses to survive.

Every decision they made meant life or death in a landscape full of dangers. Finding food and a safe place to sleep was a constant struggle against nature's challenges. Only the strongest and smartest survived.

3

Conforming to the environment wasn't just a choice; it was a necessity. Those who couldn't adapt, or who didn't understand nature's warning signs, were quickly wiped out. It was a time when every heartbeat proved the ability to overcome challenges in a wild and uncaged world.

If you think about the past thousands of years and how the human race has evolved to where we are today, you'll quickly understand why you may feel uncomfortable pursuing your biggest and wildest dreams.

We are biologically conditioned to fit in. Conforming was the only way to ensure our survival and genetic imprint into the future. Life spans and disease eradication rely heavily on our genetic ability to conform, cooperate, and combine.

Consider the people in ancient times. If someone did not fit in, not only did they not survive, but they did not find a mate. Their genes and traits died with them. So, for thousands of years, the only genes that continued were those of individuals who 'fit in'.

This type of survival of the fittest society is no longer the case because of advancements created by the human race. Modern medicine and technology have stepped in; natural selection is not what it used to be. Because of where we are now with technologies, treatments, and social changes, we no longer have to 'fit in' to advance the human race or our family's name.

So, what does that mean for us as individuals?

It means that the qualities that once spelled the difference between life and death, like conforming to the norms around us, are no longer vital. In the place of these qualities, things like healthcare, education, economic resources, and technology have become critical determinants of success and well-being in our species.

Imagine the possibilities this opens up with the evolutionary pressure to survive being taken away. As humans, we're now free to focus on what truly matters: building a life that aligns with our dreams and aspirations. We got a glimpse of this freedom during the Renaissance but were quickly ushered into offices and onto assembly lines with the Industrial Revolution. We never got the chance to take the human race to its full potential. But now, with all of our modern advancements, we have a chance to redefine our priorities and, in the process, discover what it truly means to live a fulfilling life.

We're no longer confined by the same constraints that our ancient ancestors were, including those a hundred or even fifty years ago.

## An Analogy of Adaptation: The Skill of Empathy

Until the early 21st century, empathy was commonly believed to be a fixed trait, an inborn quality that certain individuals possessed while others lacked. It was thought to be deeply ingrained in a person's nature. Some people cared about others; some did not.

However, in the early 2000s, pioneering studies conducted by neuroscientists challenged this age-old belief. Their research revealed that empathy is not a rigid, unchangeable trait but rather a skill that can be cultivated and enhanced through deliberate practice and understanding. This paradigm-shifting discovery transformed our perspective on human connections.

It was this revelation that opened the door to a new way of approaching relationships, both personal and societal. It encouraged the practice of empathy, not just as a passive feeling but as an active, intentional effort to comprehend others' emotions and experiences. As people realized the malleability of empathy, it inspired a wave of kindness, understanding, and connection, reshaping how we relate to one another on a fundamental level.

What a powerful concept. This one isolated moment in time challenges the fixed mindset surrounding human behavior, reminding us that even our most deeply ingrained beliefs could be transformed through a shift in perspective.

Just as the idea of treating everyone with kindness tells a different story than initially believed for thousands of years, our lives can be transformed when we embrace fresh perspectives and challenge our preconceived notions of how our lives should play out as well.

This paradigm shift can be the catalyst that propels us to live the life of our dreams and not just accept the life we've come to know. By re-examining our beliefs and habits, we can identify areas where change is needed, opening the door for growth and personal evolution.

We can dream.

## Life is about more than survival.

Right now, we're not doomed to merely surviving; we can thrive. But only if we choose to. Consider this empathy analogy an invitation to assess your own life.

What are the aspects of your life that would benefit from a new perspective or fresh approach? Allow yourself to say, "Hey, the way I thought my life would go, maybe that's not really it. Maybe this isn't the life that I *want*."

All this conforming and doing what you feel you're *supposed* to do isn't the answer to advancing and living the life of your dreams. You can and should live toward your purpose, desires, and passions.

## Proof of dreaming.

Consider these thought-provoking words by Elon Musk:
**"I think it's possible for ordinary people to choose to be extraordinary."**

Elon Musk, a polarizing figure to some, is clearly a man who dared to dream big. He revolutionized the electric car industry with the company, Tesla. He pioneered space exploration with SpaceX, mass internet opportunities with Starlink, co-pioneered accessible artificial intelligence with OpenAI, and one of the first online payment options with PayPal. As of this writing, he's currently pivoting Twitter into the world's first global 'free speech' platform, which he's rebranding as X.

His forward-thinking approach to business and willingness to take risks exemplify how human evolution has moved beyond mere survival and ventured into innovation and progress. Elon Musk's story is a powerful testament to what's possible when we shift our focus from simply staying alive and start to push the boundaries of what we can achieve as humans.

In the 21st century, we have witnessed other monumental breakthroughs that echo Musk's innovative spirit. CRISPR gene editing, pioneered by scientists Jennifer Doudna and Emmanuelle Charpentier, offers precise modification of genes, opening avenues for curing genetic diseases and enhancing crop resilience. Their collaborative efforts have ushered in a medical revolution, making once-incurable genetic disorders potentially treatable and promising a future where debilitating diseases could become history.

Satoshi Nakamoto, believed to be the mysterious figure behind Bitcoin, introduced blockchain technology, revolutionizing numerous industries. This decentralized ledger system ensures transparent and secure transactions, disrupting finance, supply chains, and even voting systems. Nakamoto's innovation has empowered a new era of efficient, decentralized transactions, reshaping traditional financial systems.

Figures like Geoffrey Hinton, known as the "Godfather of Deep Learning," have propelled artificial intelligence forward. His work in deep learning algorithms, inspired by the human brain, has transformed healthcare and transportation.

As a people, we are no longer constrained by survival. We can turn our attention toward the pursuit of groundbreaking ideas and the realizations of our wildest dreams. We can pursue our passions.

## What does this mean for your life?

Consider how you can channel Musk, Doudna, Charpentier, Nakamoto, and Hinton's innovative spirit and fearless determination to create the life you've always imagined for yourself. What are some areas where you have played it safe when you could have taken bold leaps toward your dreams? Do you even know what your dreams are, or are you just stuck on the hamster wheel of life?

Remember that part of the reason growth feels so uncomfortable is because, in our DNA, we are wired with the instinct that not standing out is the only way to survive. Don't separate from the pack. Hunt in groups. Huddle in the back of the cave together so the predators don't find us.

## Lessons learned from the tales of evolution and human progress

The underlying theme woven through these stories is the concept of paradigm shifts and the importance of embracing new ideas while releasing the indoctrinating beliefs and opinions of what we believe to be the world around us.

It's essential to question everything. Adaptation, optimization, and evolution are crucial to our growth and development as individuals and as a collective species.

*"We question all our beliefs, except for the ones that we truly believe, and those we never think to question."*
*- Orson Scott Card*

The beliefs that we truly hold dear are the ones that operate in the background of our minds. They are assumptions we make about how the world is and how it's supposed to be. How it "should" be. What we "have" to do.

For every belief you have, ask yourself these five questions:

1. *Where/who* did I first learn/inherit this belief from?

2. *How* is this belief serving me/or is it holding me back?

3. *Is* there a chance it might not be true?

4. *Do* I want to continue to believe this to be true?

5. *Why/why not* am I **choosing** this belief going forward?

*"I need a good paying job."*

Do you? Who says you need to have a job at all? Is this belief holding you back from pursuing your dream life? Is there even a chance you can pay your basic expenses without a 'regular' job? Do you want to keep the belief that you have to work until you die? If yes, why do you want to work until you die? If no, what would you do with your time if you weren't working all the time? Question everything!

*"I should stay in my hometown."*

Why? Because that's how it's always been done? What will happen if you leave your hometown? Is the world going to end? Will you set out on an adventure of a lifetime? Will you fail miserably and have to come crawling back? You won't know until you try, but you will go to your deathbed regretting not trying.

*"I should just stay in my unfulfilling relationship."*

Is 'not bad' good enough for you? Are you worth nothing more than a boring, mediocre life? What if the person you're destined to be with is waiting for you? What example will you set for your future children? Is staying the same advice you'd give your best friend in the same situation?

*"Jesus Christ is my savior."*

Is he? Where did this belief come from? How is it serving you? Is there a chance it's not true? Do you want to keep believing that you have a savior? If yes, why are you choosing to keep this in your life? If no, why not?

Nothing being right or wrong, just questioning everything and consciously *choosing* our beliefs. Doing enough due diligence to understand why we are choosing the beliefs we are choosing, and not blindly following any paradigm handed down to us.

When we question everything, we give ourselves the opportunity to find out one of two things:

1. Enough evidence to say "I should continue to believe in this because ___, ___, and ___."

2. Or the opposite. And once and for all we are set free from a bullish— belief system that was planted into us from someone/somewhere against our unconscious will.

Questioning everything.

*"I need that promotion."*

*"I can't fail."*

*"I'll retire when I'm sixty."*

*"I can't afford that trip."*

*"Rich people are bad."*

*"I'm waiting for my soulmate."*

*"They'll never forgive me."*

*"Millionaire by thirty."*

Sound familiar?

Where did this limiting mental chatter come from? How is it serving you? Or is it not? Is there a chance it's bullsh–? Do you want to believe this? And if yes/no, why or why not?

Chances are, if you really take a step back and think about it, these naysaying voices are not your own. They're the voices of the people who first convinced you that dreaming big was a fool's errand. Their insecurities infiltrated your peace of mind. It's time to break free from that nonsense and go after what you want!

By remaining open to new perspectives and being willing to let go of old ideas that we may not have even *chosen* to believe, we can adapt to the ever-changing world around us and unlock our full potential.

Remember that our ancestors overcame incredible odds and adapted to their environments to survive. As the descendants of these resilient individuals, we, too, can evolve and optimize our lives to pursue our dreams—and that is what they would want for us. They didn't fight to live so we could die insignificant, sad, and broke.

## Choosing Growth Over Safety

*"At any given moment, we have two options:*
*to step forward into growth or to step back into safety."*
*- Abraham Maslow*

This quote by renowned psychologist and leading personal growth and evolution expert, Abraham Maslow, perfectly encapsulates the essence of the choices we face every day, which ultimately determine our life's trajectory. Imagine each choice as a crossroads, defining the course of our lives. It's a concept we encounter daily, shaping our very existence. As we create our Dreams Lists, Maslow's simple yet profound insight becomes our guiding star.

Our focus here is on a fundamental shift in perspective—challenging deeply rooted beliefs and welcoming fresh outlooks. Maslow's wisdom reminds us that every single moment presents a choice. Opting for growth over safety is equivalent to becoming architects of our own fate. This transformation of mindset, which we'll explore in depth throughout this book, holds the key to unlocking the untapped potential within us. It's not just about reaching our goals; it's about infusing our lives with vitality, passion, and purpose in the pursuit of them.

Consider this: a study by Gallup disclosed a startling fact—only **fifteen percent** of American workers are fully engaged in their daily tasks.

Only fifteen percent of people truly and deeply care about the work they're doing on a day-to-day basis. Everyone else is going through the motions.

This revelation reaffirms our mission. In the middle of this widespread disconnect, our path becomes clear. By consciously choosing the path of growth, we not only redefine our existence but also honor the dreams of our ancestors. We are not merely envisioning a life; we are crafting a legacy, one rich in meaning and fulfillment. These choices, accessible to all, hold the transformation not just of our lives but of generations to come—a legacy of tenacity, passion, and purpose.

The study also addresses a concerning trend within the human species: rather than pursuing passions and striving for growth, many people are simply going through the motions, collecting a paycheck, and trudging along a well-trodden path toward the end of their life on earth.

## Yet, We're All Here

We are all living, we are all working, and we are all simply trying to get by. But what an exciting concept that we need to evolve further. What is the goal of life? To collect a paycheck, remain complacent, and exist within the confines of our comfort zone? Clock in and clock out ad nauseam until our time on this earth is over?

Or can we muster the courage to break free from this stagnant point and embark on a journey of growth, evolution, and passion?

The choice is *yours* to make.

## Dreaming is Necessary

In the end, the message is clear: we must not settle for survival but instead, choose to thrive in every aspect of our lives. By doing so, we enrich our existence and pave the way for future generations to continue the remarkable journey of human evolution. There's one guiding principle that I always want to come back to:

*Always be willing to learn and adapt.*

This rule of thumb is a powerful reminder that we must remain open and receptive to change, continually seeking new knowledge and experiences to expand our horizons. One of my favorite quotes is from Dan Casetta, podcast host and legendary business executive:

## "Strong beliefs, loosely held."

This quote encapsulates the idea that what we believe to be true is simply what we *believe* to be true. We should be open to the possibility of a bigger, more fulfilling life.

## Priming for Thriving

In the journey of personal development, one powerful practice that can help you choose your dreams on a daily basis is Tony Robbins's priming technique. It's not just a breathing exercise; it's a holistic approach to thriving, not just surviving.

Priming is about setting the right mindset to tackle the day. It's a practice that combines gratitude, visualization, and breathwork to create a state of focus and positivity. Imagine starting your day not just by going through the motions, but by consciously designing your emotional and mental state. That's what priming offers.

The practice begins with finding a quiet space and a comfortable posture. With eyes closed, you take deep breaths, filling your lungs and exhaling the stress of the day before. But priming is not just about the breaths; it's about cultivating gratitude.

Tony suggests recalling three specific moments of gratitude. These could be from your past, present, or even your imagined future. As you relive these moments in your mind, you let the gratitude sink in. Feel it in your body, and in your soul. This isn't just a mental exercise; it's a visceral experience.

Now comes the visualization part. You breathe in positive energy, imagining a vibrant light entering your body. With every breath, this light cleanses you, renews you. It's a moment of connection with the universe, a moment to realize your place in the grand scheme of things.

The practice concludes by celebrating victories. Not grand, life-changing victories necessarily, but the small, everyday ones. It's about appreciating the moments when you stood up to a challenge or helped someone in need. These moments of pride and courage become the foundation upon which you build your day.

Imagine starting your day with this sense of gratitude and accomplishment. Imagine carrying this positivity with you, not just in your thoughts, but in your very being. That's the essence of priming.

Incorporating priming into your routine is a habit and a mindset shift. It's a way to infuse your day with purpose and positivity, to approach challenges with resilience and opportunities with enthusiasm.

In the hustle of everyday life, it's easy to forget the power of our own minds. Priming is a reminder that each day is not just a series of tasks, but a canvas upon which you can paint your emotions, your thoughts, and your actions.

As we move forward in this journey of personal growth and the pursuit of our dreams, remember the power of priming. It's not just a technique; it's a way of being. It's a reminder that you have the power to shape your own reality, one breath at a time, one moment at a time.

## Finding the Balance Between Gratitude and Wanting More

While a sense of gratitude for what life has offered so far is important, there's a study published in the journal "Emotion" that offers compelling evidence about goal setting. It suggests that pursuing one's passion and engaging in activities that provide a sense of reaching for more in life is linked to greater well-being and happiness. According to the study, individuals who successfully identify and pursue their passions are more likely to live fulfilling and joyful lives.

While this finding may seem obvious, it underscores the importance of engaging in activities that imbue our lives with meaning and purpose. By doing so, we not only enhance our well-being and happiness but also contribute to the ongoing evolution of humanity as we collectively seek to optimize our existence.

The study is a powerful reminder that prioritizing our passions and cultivating a sense of purpose should be at the forefront of our efforts to optimize our lives. By aligning our actions with our deepest values and desires, we unlock our full potential, fostering a life filled with joy, fulfillment, and full autonomy. So, as you get started on your journey toward the life of your dreams, let this study and my rule of thumb–*Always be willing to learn and adapt*–serve as guiding lights, inspiring you to passionately pursue the activities and experiences that provide you with a sense of meaning, purpose, and *happiness*.

Happiness is not how good we feel; it's why we feel good. And by pursuing something that gives you purpose, you can feel good about what you do daily. Remember my goal on my own Dreams List? *Never feel like I'm working a day in my life.* This is how I got here.

As we reflect on that study in the journal "Emotion", it is important to consider the barriers that prevent us from fully embracing the pursuit. One of the obstacles cited by many is the belief that they don't have "enough money" to follow their passions and embark on a life of purpose and fulfillment. This shared concern raises a crucial question:

How can we overcome financial constraints and other barriers to fully embrace our passions and live the life of our dreams?

To look deeper into this question, the next chapter will explore the relationship between money and the pursuit of passions, examining strategies and insights that can help you navigate the complexities of modern life's finances and unlock the door to your Dream Life.

As we transition into the next chapter, let us carry the lessons learned so far, remaining open and adaptive to the ever-evolving landscape of our lives and steadfast in our commitment to growth, evolution, and pursuing our deepest passions.

# CHAPTER 2

# "I Don't Have the Money"

**M**any people think, 'I'll start dreaming when I have more time and money.' But, as I've proven in my own life, dream achievement is a function of intentionality and habits. Not bankroll. If you wait until you already have the money to fund your dreams, one of two things will happen.

You won't ever get *enough*. There will always be another peak of the money mountain you need to summit before you'll let yourself dream.

Or, you'll suddenly find yourself with money and no purpose, leading to a fool and his money being soon parted.

Before we can dive into our quest to build our Dream Life, we must first explore the barriers that have prevented us from fully embracing our passions and pursuing the Life of our Dreams so far and this chapter is a journey into the intricate relationship between money and our deepest desires. We'll explore practical strategies and profound insights to navigate the complex world of modern finances and unlock the door to the life we've always envisioned.

Hold tight; this chapter is not just about facts and figures. It's about self-discovery, empathy, and personal growth. It's about understanding the origins of our financial beliefs and reshaping our views on wealth and abundance.

As we dig into the world of financial beliefs, I am going to use a hypothetical man named Cameron. Remember that this is not just Cameron's story; it's our story. It's a narrative that resonates with countless individuals who, like our new friend Cameron, have grappled with the belief that they don't have enough *money* to chase their dreams. It's a tale of how our upbringing, experiences, and the society we live in shape our beliefs about money, shaping our paths as adults.

So, if you've ever found yourself uttering the words, "I don't have enough money to…," or "If I had the money, I'd…" or if you've witnessed others wrestling with this issue, this chapter is your compass. By the time we're through, you will gain insights into your financial beliefs, and you'll uncover the tools and inspiration to conquer financial constraints and step confidently onto the path of purpose and fulfillment.

## Meet 'Cameron'

Once upon a time, in a world not so different from our own, there lived a man named Cameron. Cameron grew up in a middle class family where money was sometimes tight and practical choices had to be made about where to allocate funds. He went to college for four years, mostly to play college baseball, and planned to use his business degree to someday take over the concrete company he works for. He is a dedicated worker, a soon-to-be loving husband—a model of middle-class respectability. Yet, there is a shadow looming over Cameron's life, a belief that whispers in the back of his mind: "I don't have enough money."

Notice that Cameron's story isn't unique. It's a story that echoes through the lives of most of us. It's a tale of beliefs and behavior, a theme that resonates even among those who have achieved great financial success. A Harvard study asked a room filled with millionaires how much more money would make them feel truly free to pursue their deepest desires. The answer was revealing:

**For those who already had a net worth of $1M, they said double.**

**Those with $2M? They, too, desired double.**

**Even those with $4M in net worth— the same response—double.**

**Astonishingly, even at the lofty sum of $10M, the answer remained just about the same. Double.**

This chapter isn't about how much money you have; it's about the beliefs that shape your relationship with money. For our example, Cameron, these beliefs trace their roots back to his childhood—a time when money was in short supply, or at least so he thought. This scarcity mindset became Cameron's guiding mantra, influencing his choices and actions throughout the rest of his life.

One day, when Cameron was ten years old, he asked his parents for new baseball cleats, and the response was, "Sorry, Cameron, we can't afford them."

For the rest of his life, this idea took hold. "There's not enough money for what I want."

What Cameron, and probably his parents, failed to recognize was that dad had a $5,000 lawn mower and mom was leasing a car with a payment of $300/month. The day before, they took a family trip to Costco, which cost $30 in gas, $20 for coffee on the way, and $400 at checkout. Then, they stopped for family dinner and settled for a 'cheap' $80 meal (after tip) at Applebees.

Not having "enough money" had nothing to do with Cameron getting baseball cleats; it was all about where that money was being spent. Yet, for the rest of his life, it was moments like *these*–moments his parents probably wouldn't even remember–that shaped the way he would look at money forever.

I was recently at Disney World, where I watched a six-year-old ask her mom, "Can I *please* get *both* ($80) backpacks?"

Her mom's response was, "Honey, we can't afford that."

Little did this girl know that the flights were $600, hotel $500, park passes $400, food $100/day, etc for each member of the family. And yet, for the rest of her life, she will have internalized that her family "couldn't afford" things.

But let us not forget that Cameron's story, and this little girl's story, is our story, illustrating how deeply ingrained beliefs about money, often stemming from our earliest years, shape our identities and guide our life pursuits. Cameron grew up in a family that, while not impoverished, always felt the weight of financial scarcity. This perception of monetary limitations became Cameron's core financial understanding, molding his daily choices and actions for life.

## Financial Psychology and Lessons From History

To illustrate the point that money is less about facts and figures, and more about psychology and beliefs, let's take a trip back to ancient Egypt and explore the life of one of history's most iconic figures, Cleopatra. As one of the wealthiest women in history, Cleopatra had access to vast resources and wielded immense power. Despite her wealth, she faced financial challenges that ultimately contributed to her downfall.

Cleopatra's fortune came first from her inheritance and then from her efforts. Her father was a great ruler who passed down fertile lands, gold mines, and strategic trade routes that Cleopatra expanded and built upon. Yet, despite her considerable riches,

Cleopatra's reign was marred by a series of financial hardships that would erode her authority and culminate in tragedy.

Her most daunting financial hurdle was the colossal debt she inherited from her father upon ascending to the throne. Remarkably, Cleopatra's experience isn't entirely dissimilar to that of wealthy and prominent figures who embark on their adult lives today.

Take, for instance, the case of Donald Trump, another polarizing figure, for sure. His financial narrative bears a resemblance to Cleopatra's, marked by a multitude of assets and debts that originated with a "small loan" of $1M from his father. Trump transformed this somewhat modest starting point into a substantial fortune, with an estimated net worth of $4.6B before his presidential bid in 2016, primarily by skillfully leveraging debt. To merely cover his annual mortgage payments, Trump would need to accomplish a staggering volume of business. It is estimated that in 1995, his business incurred over $900M in expenses, and by the 2010s carried over $400M in debts.

Cleopatra's narrative shares a common theme. Despite her substantial inheritance, her reign was haunted by debts passed down from her father, debts she opted to disregard. Because she hadn't created the debts, she failed to recognize them as a burden, embracing lavish spending and reinforcing her perception that money was an infinite resource at her disposal.

This belief, rooted in the ignorance of what she perceived as an unlimited resource, led her to make risky and costly political alliances with Julius Caesar and Mark Antony, marked by extravagant displays of wealth and excess intended to secure her power and support. However, these alliances proved her undoing, as they alienated powerful factions in Rome and contributed to her eventual downfall.

Her story is a cautionary tale about how our beliefs about money shape our financial success or lack thereof. Because of her vast wealth, she believed that money was unlimited, a belief inherited from her upbringing. This mindset led her to make costly mistakes, resulting in her tragic end.

Cleopatra's story is a powerful example of how our relationships with money and our beliefs can impact our financial outcomes.

## Money Beliefs of Another Prominent Figure

I've purposely used two examples of historical figures that had a problem with too *much* money to illustrate that no matter what financial bracket someone is in, the underlying beliefs that aren't noticed or addressed will always lead to their demise. I understand that 99% of people aren't in a financial position like Donald Trump or Cleopatra, which is exactly why this section is for you and is necessary before even considering putting pen to paper in creating your Dreams List.

Martha Stewart, a celebrated businesswoman and television personality, is another example of money belief systems leading to money problems. She basked in the limelight of success for a significant portion of her life, particularly during the 1990's and became an American icon, reshaping the concept of home life and symbolizing affluence.

However, the early 2000s ushered in a stark reversal of fortune when Martha found herself embroiled in a scandal centered around insider trading. This crisis threatened her entire empire, leading to her conviction and a five-month sentence in federal prison. Behind bars, Martha underwent a profound period of self-reflection, confronting her beliefs and attitudes that had long shaped her financial decisions.

During this time of introspection, she came to a stark realization. Her relentless pursuit of perfectionism, the need for excessive control, and the insatiable desire for more money had put everything she truly valued at risk. It was a sobering awakening, made all the more impactful by the cold environment of prison walls around her.

Stewart's time behind bars became the crucible in which she forged a new perspective on money, one that aligned with her evolving values. While it's easy to cast judgment, we must remember that we all make choices with consequences. Whether it's sacrificing time with loved ones for work, taking extra shifts for more money, or accepting a job that doesn't resonate with our passion or purpose solely for financial gain, these decisions often stem from our money beliefs.

Martha's story serves as an extreme reminder that our beliefs about money come with consequences when not addressed or rewired.

## Examining Our Money Beliefs

In his book *Secrets of the Millionaire Mind*, T. Harv Eker discusses common money myths that can limit our financial success. Addressing and identifying the following myths can reshape your money blueprint and develop a more prosperous mindset.

1. Money is limited.

2. Money is the root of all evil.

3. If you're making money, you're taking it from somebody else.

4. Money makes you a worse person.

5. Money can't buy happiness.

## Dispelling Money Myths

To break down these common money myths, we need a few key insights:

1. Money is not limited. While some believe money is scarce, the truth is, it's nearly boundless. This isn't to say your own personal account is limitless…yet. Only that there's enough in the world to go around. In 2020 alone, the government injected roughly $5 trillion into our economy, and this doesn't even include the money printed in 2023 after the FTX Bank collapse. Money is continually circulating, with new bills printed daily. The question isn't whether money is limited, but rather, "How can I attract more money to myself?" With the

growing popularity of cryptocurrencies and other *forms* of "money", this has never been more true.

2. Money itself isn't evil. It's a neutral tool. It's the people who use it for good or bad purposes. Money magnifies your true nature, so if you're already good-hearted, more money can enable you to do more good, like giving to that GoFundMe campaign to help a local family in need. Some people will give their last dollar to help another. Give that person more money, and the chances of them sharing the wealth would only increase.

3. Making money isn't taking it from others. Money is in a constant exchange, always flowing. Just because someone spends money with you doesn't make you a bad person. If not with you, they'd spend it elsewhere. Money represents value exchanged. If you purchase a high-end, American-made product, that money circulates through the pockets of employees, vendors, and manufacturers. On a large enough scale, commerce alone goes a long way toward keeping the country running. It's only when those at the top hoard the money they receive instead of recirculating it through the economy, that we see it being taken from others.

4. Money doesn't inherently change you for the worse. It amplifies who you are. If you have personal issues or pain, address them; money won't solve them. If you're already happy and purposeful, more money will enhance your fulfillment. Many celebrities and lottery winners

find this out the hard way and embark on their journey toward fulfillment much later in life, after already achieving the only goal they had set for themselves.

5. Money can't directly buy happiness, but it can buy things and opportunities that bring joy. It also provides time and freedom, enhancing comfort. The notion that "money can't buy happiness" is often voiced by those with limited financial means. Consider for a moment, a father with limited means using a bonus or raise to purchase a lawn care or cleaning service so he and his wife could give that time back to their four kids. He's not only bringing joy to his family, but funneling money into two service providers who are probably small business owners themselves. In this one example, at least eight lives are positively impacted by that one financial decision.

## Transforming Money Beliefs

Money doesn't change you for the worse; it magnifies your true nature. If you're content and purposeful, more money will enhance your fulfillment.

Money doesn't directly buy happiness, but it can acquire things that boost happiness and provide freedom, increasing comfort.

Identifying and changing these limiting beliefs is key to abundance. The path to unlocking your financial potential involves dispelling these money myths and working toward your ideal life. It all begins with self-awareness.

Take action, assess your beliefs, and affirm those that support abundance.

To unlock your financial potential, replace limiting beliefs with positive affirmations. For instance, instead of saying, "Money is the root of all evil," say, "Money is a tool that allows me to create a positive impact in the world."

Additional positive money affirmations to consider include:

- ◆ "Money flows effortlessly and abundantly into my life."

- ◆ "I am worthy of financial success and prosperity."

- ◆ "My wealth grows as I continue to provide value to the world."

- ◆ "I attract financial opportunities and abundance with an open heart and mind."

- ◆ "Financial abundance allows me to create the life I desire."

- ◆ "I am in control of my finances, and I make wise financial decisions."

- ◆ "Money is a reflection of the value I bring to others."

- ◆ "I release any fear or guilt associated with wealth and welcome abundance into my life."

- ◆ "I am grateful for the abundance that surrounds me."

◆ "I use my wealth to make a positive difference in the world."

These affirmations can help reshape your money beliefs and pave the way for a more abundant and fulfilling financial journey.

## Transforming Your Money Blueprint

Addressing and altering these limiting beliefs is crucial for abundance. The key to unlocking your financial potential lies in dispelling these myths and pursuing your ideal life. Self-awareness is the first step—recognize and confront the beliefs holding you back. Replace limiting beliefs with positive affirmations that promote abundance.

### Steps to Reinforce Money Beliefs

1. Take action.

2. Assess your beliefs.

3. Reinforce beliefs that nurture abundance.

4. Evaluate your current position and envision your future in ten years.

5. Examine whether your circumstances and environment support or hinder your financial goals.

*"Income can only grow as much as you do."*
*- T. Harv Eker*

To achieve significant financial success, invest in personal growth and reshape your money beliefs. Develop a positive association between money and success, as viewing financial success as attainable and positive is crucial. Building wealth becomes challenging if you despise wealthy individuals.

## Understanding the Value Exchange

Consider the value exchange in financial transactions. Take an athlete like Patrick Mahomes, for example. He recently signed a $500M contract, with $213M guaranteed, to be the quarterback for the Kansas City Chiefs. Does he deserve it? Let's do the math.

The Chiefs pay him from revenue sources like ticket sales, TV deals, jersey sales, and advertising sponsors. Digging into advertising sponsors, the Chiefs generated $1.4B from them last year.

Is it worth it for sponsors to invest in a team with one of the world's top sports superstars? They're banking on the fact that by paying him this high rate, he will, in turn, bring fans to the stadium and the stores with money ready to spend. This showcases the depth of value exchanged.

But let's scale down to a teacher making $30,000 annually. Who pays the teacher? The school district. And where does that money come from? Taxpayers. Is it worthwhile for taxpayers to contribute to the teacher's salary? For some, the teacher brings little perceived value, but for those with students in that school, the teacher provides education and time spent on their child's development, which holds a ton of value. Even for those living in the community who do not have children of their own, the salary they're contributing to goes toward educating future members of their same society, which does hold some value.

Every individual values things uniquely. What I spend my money on may be crazy to you, and vice versa. If a sixteen-year-old knew that the rug in the living room cost their mom five hundred dollars, they would go crazy when mom says, "We can't afford the Nike cleats". Our perception of *cost* changes in regard to our current values.

But when someone desires more income, they must bring more "value" to the *marketplace* as a whole. If you earn less, don't resent those who earn more; they're simply creating more monetary value in the world as a whole, and their paychecks and bank accounts reflect that. I believe teachers make a huge impact on human lives, but I don't think anyone would argue the fact that those students won't be creating monetary value in the world for many years. When you compare the short-term monetary value of a group of fourth graders to the immediate monetary value created by selling three office buildings, it makes it very obvious as to why it's so hard to convince the government to pay teachers more.

## Understanding Wealth Beyond Money

As you shift your mindset from negative money beliefs to empowering affirmations, it's crucial to deepen your understanding of wealth and its distinction from money. This is where Paul Graham's insightful essay "How to Make Wealth" sheds light on the essence of true wealth. Graham presents wealth as the broader tapestry of resources that enhance our lives—encompassing not just the money in our wallets but everything we value, from the essentials like food and shelter to the joys of exploring new destinations.

Wealth, according to Graham, is the core of our desires, the sum of our aspirations. It is about the quality of life, not just the quantity of currency. When we speak of wealth, we're referring to the richness of our experiences, the depth of our engagements, and the breadth of our satisfactions. It's a concept that transcends the monetary and taps into the qualitative essence of what makes life truly meaningful.

Money, on the other hand, is merely a conduit, a mechanism through which we move wealth. It's the common language of exchange that enables us to transfer value from one to another. But it's not the wealth itself. Graham eloquently debunks the 'Pie Fallacy,' the misguided belief that wealth is finite, like a pie that, once divided, leaves less for others. He clarifies that wealth is not static or limited. It is a dynamic force that can be created, expanded, and multiplied through innovation, creativity, and value addition. For instance, when you restore an old car, you're not taking away from someone else's slice of the pie; you're baking a whole new pie. In doing so, you create wealth, enhancing not just your own life but contributing to the wealth of the world at large. When explained like this, the pie fallacy almost seems foolish. The power of our belief systems.

Graham's insights align with Dan Sullivan's philosophy in "10X is Easier than 2X," which also views wealth as qualitative and synonymous with freedom. Sullivan suggests that wealth is reflected in the value and quality of four key life aspects: your time, your money, your relationships, and your overall purpose. By focusing on these areas, wealth becomes more than a financial measure—it becomes a reflection of a life well-lived, rich in experiences, and imbued with personal growth and freedom.

## Five Pillars of Wealth Creation

Managing money effectively is essential for achieving financial stability and success in today's fast-paced world. However, many aren't tracking expenses and crafting solid financial plans as they should. Let's dive into the valuable insights that will empower you to take control of your finances and reshape your wealth mindset.

*1. Rewire Your Thinking About Money:*

Step one is transforming your perspective on money. It involves examining your fundamental beliefs and attitudes about wealth and finance and making changes to develop a healthier and more positive relationship with money. By doing this, you aim to create a mindset that aligns with your financial goals and helps you make better financial decisions. It's a personal journey of self-discovery and transformation in how you view and manage your finances.

*2. Shifting Focus to Net Worth:*

A critical aspect of wealth is that it is a focus and concentration on net worth instead of merely the bank account balance. While the bank balance offers a snapshot of your current financial situation, net worth encompasses total assets and liabilities. Tracking and growing your net worth provides a more accurate representation of your overall financial health.

### 3. Surrounding Yourself With Success:

Another vital piece of wealth building is the significance of associating with positive and successful people. Successful individuals often surround themselves with like-minded individuals who inspire and motivate them to strive for greatness. Cultivating a supportive and uplifting network can grant valuable insights and opportunities that accelerate your financial growth. I pride myself on getting in "the rooms where it happens." Always be the smallest person in the room. Get into rooms where you feel like an imposter. Get into networks where those around you make you feel massively uncomfortable. Learning the language of money is like learning another speaking language. If you are around rich people and don't understand what they're talking about, you are in the right room. Start to learn the language and embody the wealthy's actions and habits.

### 4. Getting Paid for Value:

Wealthy and less affluent people have differing views on earning money. Wealthy individuals recognize the importance of being compensated for the value they bring to the world. Rather than solely trading time for money, they seek ways to provide value and make a meaningful impact. By shifting your mindset and identifying how you can contribute value, you can unlock new avenues for financial growth and prosperity.

5. *The Power of Tracking:*

I believe it is crucial for anyone attempting to be successful in anything to track everything. In the case of money, that includes income, expenses, and net worth. The spreadsheet tool that I created for myself includes three tabs: "Net Worth Tracker", "Liquid Money/Savings Tracker", and "Cash Flow Tracker." (All templates found on my website alexrfunk.com for FREE)

For expenses, this is an absolute necessity. If you don't know where your money is going, you will never be able to re-allocate it towards your dreams. A pro-tip for you: stop using cash. It is untraceable. You need to see that you spent $140 at the bar on Friday night to feel the appropriate regret. You need to realize that the $400 you've spent on Chipotle this winter could have funded a round-trip flight to Vegas. Tracking these things is a must. You must demonstrate the ability to manage $100 before you can expect to handle $1,000. And this principle holds true at every level up to and beyond dealing with millions of dollars.

For net worth, put in bank account balances, credit card amounts, loans, and investments. My personal tracker also has a fourth tab titled percentage-based budgeting, which enables commission-based or business owners a chance at budgeting based on specific percentages of their income to various categories, such as necessities, dreams, and savings. This systematic approach ensures that funds are appropriately allocated, and financial goals are prioritized.

By rewiring your money mindset, focusing on net worth, surrounding yourself with success-oriented individuals, getting compensated for the value you provide, and utilizing the shared spreadsheet with percentage-based budgeting, you can transform your financial journey.

Whether you're at the Trump and Stewart financial level to start off, or closer to that teacher's salary, or lower, get in the habit of thinking like the rich when it comes to your money. Take control of your finances, establish a solid financial plan, and step into a future of financial freedom. Remember, there is always an opportunity to master your money-tracking skills and pave the way to wealth. Let's embark on this journey together and build a prosperous financial future and the life of our dreams.

## Time: The True Currency

While our perception of wealth and money significantly impacts our financial success and abundance, we must also consider another finite resource often overlooked: time. Unlike money, which can be earned and re-earned, time is non-renewable; it runs out. With this in mind, let's explore how our beliefs and attitudes toward time influence our ability to achieve our dreams in Chapter 3.

# CHAPTER 3
## "I Don't Have the Time"

Imagine a world where each tick of the clock is a priceless gem, a fleeting moment that, once gone, can never be reclaimed. This is the world we live in, yet we often forget the immense value of time, the true currency of life.

Greek philosopher Theophrastus once said, 'Time is the most valuable thing a man can spend.' Yet, in the hustle of our daily lives, especially for those in high-pressure roles, those in the daily routines of their nine-to-five jobs, and young adults carving out their paths, this river of time seems to slip through our fingers, unnoticed and unappreciated. We often catch ourselves in a refrain all too familiar: 'I just don't have the time.' This chapter is a deep dive into this conundrum, a quest to unravel the true value of time like those who live the lives of go-getters and dreamers.

## Days Are Numbered

Let's give Cameron from Chapter 2 a break and picture Jake, a twenty-something commission-based sales rep from a small town, now thrust into the throbbing heart of a bustling city. His days are a whirlwind of client meetings, cold calls, and relentless networking. For Jake, time is a currency more precious than any commission check, yet it always seems to be in short supply. Amidst his ambitious pursuit of success, Jake's personal passions and dreams have taken a back seat, blurred by the breakneck speed of his professional life. But one evening, as Jake sat alone in his apartment, a stark realization dawned on him. In his relentless chase for the next sale, when did he last chase his own dreams?

This pivotal moment led Jake to reassess his relationship with time. He began scrutinizing his daily routine, hunting for lost hours consumed by unproductive habits and trivial distractions. To his surprise, he discovered pockets of time, previously surrendered to aimless scrolling on social media or binge-watching shows. Jake decided to reclaim these moments, dedicating them to his long-neglected love for music. Gradually, he carved out a space for his passion amidst the chaos, enrolling in a guitar class and reigniting a dream he forgot he had as a kid.

Jake's story is emblematic of the challenges and opportunities faced by many who are lost in the daily routine of their profession. It's a tale that resonates with anyone who has ever felt overwhelmed by the demands of a fast-paced career, yet yearns for more – more fulfillment, more passion, more life. This chapter invites you to embark on a journey of time transformation, exploring effective strategies to harness this elusive resource. We'll explore how to identify and capitalize on hidden opportunities in our daily schedules, turning the ever-present 'not enough time' into a wellspring of moments that fuel our dreams and ambitions.

Our mission is to learn how to make time an ally in our quest for a fulfilling life, much like Jake discovered in his journey. This exploration will reveal the often-overlooked potential lying dormant within our daily routines, waiting to be harnessed for our dreams and aspirations.

As we navigate this exploration, let's keep in mind a poignant reminder from H. Jackson Brown, a renowned American author:

> *'Don't say you don't have enough time. You have the same hours in the day given to Helen Keller, Michelangelo, Mother Teresa, Leonardo da Vinci, Thomas Jefferson, and Albert Einstein.'*

This powerful statement urges us to reflect on how we use our time, reminding us that the key to unlocking our fullest potential is not in seeking more hours, but in optimizing the ones we have.

## Exploring Time and Duality: The Diverse Paths of Emily and Marcus

As you navigate the complexities of your life, particularly if you find yourself in a high-pressure role or in the midst of your transformative twenties, consider the stories of Emily and

Marcus. They don't directly represent you, but their experiences echo the challenges and opportunities you might face in balancing ambition with the demands of everyday life.

## Emily's Structured World

Meet Emily, whose life mirrors a well-orchestrated symphony of routine and structure. From dawn till dusk, her schedule is a testament to organization and predictability. This disciplined approach brings a sense of security and order to her life. Yet, beneath this surface of calm, you might relate to Emily's underlying dreams and unexplored passions. She enjoys the safety her routine offers but often wonders about the exciting possibilities that stepping out of her comfort zone might bring. Like Emily, you might find yourself yearning for more despite the comfort of stability.

## Marcus' World of Adventure

In contrast, Marcus embodies the essence of adventure and the pursuit of dreams. His life is a dynamic canvas of risks and rewards, reflecting the journey from the known to the unknown. His career is not just a job; it's a series of daring goals and exciting ventures. His story might resonate with you if you're drawn to the thrill of the unknown and the satisfaction of overcoming challenges. Marcus' path, with its uncertainties and pressures, brings the exhilaration of personal growth and the joy of pursuing significant ambitions, but there is little predictability and safety.

# The Trade-offs in Your Choices

The lives of Emily and Marcus highlight the trade-offs in the paths you might choose. Emily's structured life offers peace and predictability, but you might share her craving for excitement and self-discovery. Marcus, meanwhile, might inspire you with his adventurous spirit, even though his path is laced with uncertainties and pressures.

## Mastering Your Time

This brings to mind Lao Tzu's wise words: "Time is a created thing. To say 'I don't have time' is saying 'I don't want to.'" This quote challenges you to rethink your relationship with time. It's a call to reevaluate how you allocate your time, encouraging you to align your schedule with your true aspirations and values.

As we explore the concept of life's duality, let Emily and Marcus's experiences guide you. Their stories serve as a powerful reminder that the way you manage your time and the decisions you make are reflective of what you value most. These narratives set the stage to understand how to balance the comfort of the known with the thrill of the unknown, crafting a fulfilling life that resonates with your deepest desires and dreams.

## The Duality of Life

The obvious way to buy back your time is to pay someone to do something for you. Pay the mechanic to change your oil or a dry cleaner to press your suit.

The less obvious way to buy back your time is to say no. Passing on a promotion might "buy" you more time with family. Declining the dinner invite might "pay" for the time you need to exercise. We buy back our time not only with the money we spend, but also with the opportunities we decline.

*"The more clearly you know how you want to spend your days, the easier it becomes to say no to the requests that steal your hours."*
**- James Clear**

Understanding how to manage your time goes beyond just maximizing productivity and achieving goals. It's about striking a delicate balance between the pleasures and pains that life invariably presents. Here's how you can harness effective time management and intentional decision-making to not only reach your aspirations but also to enhance your overall life satisfaction.

First, consider time management as a tool for prioritizing what truly matters. It's about choosing activities that not only drive you toward your goals but also bring you joy and satisfaction. Allocate specific time blocks for tasks that are essential for your professional growth and personal development. However, also ensure you carve out time for activities that bring you pleasure and relaxation. This balance prevents burnout and maintains your enthusiasm and energy for your pursuits.

Secondly, embrace the concept of intentional decision-making. Every choice you make has the potential to add to your life's pleasure or pain. When faced with a decision, weigh the immediate outcomes against how it aligns with your long-term objectives and personal well-being. This might mean saying no to certain opportunities that, while tempting, could lead to stress or over-commitment. It's about being mindful of your decisions and how they impact your overall happiness and productivity.

By acknowledging and embracing life's inherent duality of pain and pleasure, you can approach your time with a deeper sense of purpose. This mindset allows you to make more informed choices, ensuring that your activities contribute positively to both your professional achievements and personal happiness. The goal is to create a life that balances ambition with contentment, drive with relaxation, ultimately leading to a rich, well-rounded existence.

## Achieving Balance: The Ancient Wisdom of Eudaimonia

The concept of duality in life is not a new one. Ancient Greek philosophers believed in *eudaimonia*, or the pursuit of a good life. This included pain and pleasure, with the idea that a life without either was not fulfilling. Eudaimonia, derived from the Greek words "eu-" (good) and "daimon" (spirit), is often translated as a human flourishing or living a life worth living. The ancient Greeks believed that one must embrace both the positive and negative aspects of life, recognizing that a truly fulfilling existence is composed of both.

The ancient Greek concept of eudaimonia isn't just about seeking pleasure or shunning pain; it's about finding a meaningful equilibrium in life. Eudaimonia suggests a state of flourishing that is only possible when you embrace the full spectrum of life's experiences. Aristotle, the ancient philosopher, also taught that true contentment arises from a harmony of virtues such as courage, wisdom, and temperance.

Now, consider the modern dilemma of 'not enough time.' When you say you're too busy for something, it's often an unconscious admission that it's not a priority for you. Recognizing this empowers you to reassess how you value and utilize your time. It's about making a strategic choice to incorporate activities that resonate with your core values and bring authentic joy and fulfillment into your life.

You're invited to treat time as you would a financial budget, where you allocate resources to areas that yield the most significant return in happiness and growth. This isn't a one-time adjustment but a continuous process of self-examination and realignment, ensuring that your daily actions are in sync with your deeper aspirations.

To live a life that's both satisfying and true to your values, start by identifying what genuinely matters to you. Prioritize these elements, and intentionally carve out time for them in your schedule. By doing so, you're not just living; you're thriving, in accordance with the timeless wisdom of eudaimonia.

## Pain and Pleasure

In the quest to construct your Dream Life, understanding the dance between pain and pleasure is essential. This duality isn't just philosophical—it's practical, especially when it comes to managing your time effectively. To achieve the life you envision, you must navigate through moments of both hardship and joy, recognizing that the pursuit of pleasure often involves enduring pain. The balance you strike between these experiences is crucial, not just for momentary happiness but for long-lasting fulfillment.

Consider the choices you make on a typical Friday night as a vivid illustration of this principle. Opting for the immediate high of going out and enjoying drinks with friends might seem appealing, but it often results in a next-day low, where productivity suffers, and you feel less than your best. It's a clear example of short-term pleasure potentially leading to longer-term pain—a cycle that can disrupt your time management and delay your progress toward your goals.

Now, picture the alternative: choosing the pain of discipline by turning in early and rising at dawn for a workout. This decision might require the sacrifice of immediate gratification, but it pays dividends in the euphoria and energy boost that follows a morning exercise routine. It's the pain of discipline that sets the stage for a day filled with productivity and the pleasure of accomplishment. By managing your time to prioritize these constructive activities, you ensure that your days align with your aspirations and contribute to building the Dream Life you're chasing.

By incorporating such deliberate choices into your time management strategy, you're not just passively experiencing life's ups and downs; you're actively steering your journey toward the life you desire. The ancient wisdom of eudaimonia encourages us to embrace both the positive and negative, but in doing so, it's important to recognize that choosing short-term discomfort can lead to long-term happiness and success. This understanding allows you to navigate the complexities of life with resilience and to savor the moments of joy and satisfaction that come from pursuing your dreams with intention and purpose.

Thus, the mastery of your time is deeply connected to how you manage the interplay of pain and pleasure. It's about making conscious decisions that balance your day-to-day actions with your ultimate life goals. Embrace the lows as necessary precursors to the highs, and plan your time with the knowledge that the most significant achievements often come from the most challenging efforts. This is the essence of building a life that's not only productive but also rich with meaning and joy.

However, and this is a big one, forever denying yourself a chance to unwind is as detrimental to your overall well-being as constant all-night ragers. We all know the saying, "All work and no play makes Jack a dull boy." I don't want you to be Jack, either. I believe that we choose our sacrifices at all times. What are you sacrificing and what for?

## Embracing the Flow in the Journey of Life

Flow, a concept pioneered by psychologist Mihaly Csikszentmihalyi, represents those moments where time seems to stand still, where you are so engrossed in an activity that the world around you fades away. This state of flow is more than just deep concentration; it's a harmony of engagement that elevates your happiness, bolsters productivity, and fosters personal growth.

It's in these moments of flow that you often find the balance between life's ebb and flow of pleasure and pain, and it's these moments that can redefine your journey, aligning it with your passions and the dreams you dare to chase.

It's important to take with you the understanding that achieving a state of flow can be a powerful catalyst for living a life that's not just busy, but rich with meaning. It's a life where time management transcends the mere ticking of a clock and becomes a canvas for creating your Dream Life. In what activities or areas of life do you feel yourself being in flow state? How can you get more of that in your daily routines?

## The Power of Goals and "The Strangest Secret"

As you prepare to close this chapter and learn about the strangest secret in success, consider yourself at the threshold of a deeper understanding. Here, you are ready to explore how the silent undercurrents of your thoughts and beliefs can sculpt your life's narrative. Setting goals is more than chasing ambitions; it's about charting a course, a deliberate act of steering your life through its myriad twists and turns. The concepts of flow and duality you've encountered here are your groundwork for what lies ahead—a journey where effective time management and the pursuit of your dreams coalesce to guide you forward.

In the following pages, you will discover the profound impact of aligning your innermost thoughts with your outward actions to cultivate a life that resonates with purpose and passion. The lessons learned here about balancing the dualities of life will now illuminate your path to setting and achieving goals. You are not merely moving from one chapter to the next; you are transitioning into a new phase of your journey, where you can apply the art of time management to live out your dreams in full color. Prepare to embrace the strategies that will allow you to navigate toward your most significant achievements and the everyday pleasures that make life truly worth living.

# CHAPTER 4
# "The Strangest Secret" to a Significant Life

In 1956, Earl Nightingale introduced a concept that would revolutionize personal development. His recording, "The Strangest Secret," hinged on a powerful premise: "We become what we think about." This profound idea, that our thoughts lay the groundwork for our destiny, has since guided countless individuals toward crafting lives filled with passion, purpose, and significance.

## Shaping Our Lives

Up to this point, we've journeyed through the evolution of human aspiration, unraveling your beliefs about time and money, and the critical role your choices play in leading a life brimming with vibrancy and contrast. Now, we turn the page to a concept that weaves these ideas together: the transformative power of our thoughts and beliefs.

Nightingale's revelation offered a stark, unclouded truth: the quality of your life is ultimately forged by the quality of your thoughts. Amidst the daily grind, this 'strangest secret' emerges not just as a passing insight but as a vital instrument of change—a tool that's straightforward in its message but monumental in its effect.

Now, meet Chris—a man who, like many, felt chained to a job that filled his bank account but emptied his spirit. A safe bet for sure, especially for someone from a modest beginning aiming high. Mornings for Chris were a monotonous march into a day devoid of zeal. Yes, the money was decent, but it weighed him down like an anchor, dragging him away from the dreams he yearned to chase.

But then, Earl Nightingale's "The Strangest Secret" found its way to Chris, and with it, a new dawn broke. The message was a catalyst, igniting a spark within him. He recognized how his life, clouded by routine and comfort, was actually being shaped by the subtle influences around him—the news channels that buzzed in the background, the music that filled the silence, the conversations that filled his days. They were infiltrating his thoughts, dictating the direction of his life, steering him away from the pursuit of his dreams.

With a newfound clarity, Chris took control of his narrative. He turned off the TV, silenced the background noise, and instead, invested that time into journaling his dreams, mapping out the desires he had kept dormant. This wasn't a mere tweak in his routine, but a complete overhaul of his mental landscape, igniting a revolution in his life. Empowered by a clear vision, Chris began to live with intention. He replaced hours of passive consumption with active creation, laying the groundwork for a new future.

Gradually, Chris's life began to change. Fueled by a renewed sense of direction, Chris mustered the bravery to step away from the security of his old job, embarking on a quest to fulfill his true ambitions.

Chris's transformation exemplifies the essence of "The Strangest Secret." Awareness of his inner narrative allowed him to rewrite it, aligning his reality with the aspirations that resonated deep within him. His story is not just a tale of change; it's a testament to the principle that with thought as your compass, you can navigate through life's uncertainties and sail toward a life that's not only significant but truly your own.

## Why Has Our Reality Remained Largely Unchanged?

In Earl Nightingale's "The Strangest Secret," he presents a startling statistic regarding the fate of people in our society by the time they reach retirement age, based on statistical averages. According to Nightingale, the breakdown is as follows:

◆ 54% will be broke and dependent on friends, family, or the government for financial support.

◆ 36% will be dead.

◆ 5% will still be working.

◆ 4% will be financially independent.

◆ 1% will be truly wealthy.

What's remarkable about this statistic is that it was true in 1956 when Nightingale first delivered his talk, and it remains largely true today. Despite technological advances and the increase in available information, most people still struggle to achieve financial independence and live fulfilling lives. Ninety-five percent of people today still end up poor.

This raises the question: Why has this reality remained unchanged for over half a century despite all the advances in technology, medicine, and the world around us? We have access to more knowledge and resources than ever before. Why do so many people still struggle to create a life of abundance and purpose?

## The Answer: Our Thoughts and Beliefs

According to Nightingale and many others who have since built upon his work, the answer lies in our thoughts and beliefs about ourselves and our potential. "The Strangest Secret" suggests that it's not a lack of information or resources that holds us back but the limitations we impose on ourselves through our thoughts.

It's our mindset and beliefs that can transform our potential in this one life that we get.

As Nightingale himself said:

**"The only person who succeeds is the person who is progressively realizing a worthy ideal."**

In other words, the key to achieving the life of our dreams is having a clear vision of what we want that life to look like and consistently taking daily steps toward it. This process begins in our mind.

Suppose we allow ourselves to be consumed by negative thoughts, doubts, and fears. In that case, we will likely find ourselves stuck in the same patterns that have held us back for generations. But if we can harness the power of our thoughts, beliefs, and actions, we can break free from these limitations and join the ranks of the one percent who achieve true wealth, success, and passion.

Ultimately, "The Strangest Secret" is a simple yet profound truth: *We become what we think about.* By recognizing the immense power of our thoughts and consciously directing them toward our goals and dreams, we can create a life of abundance, purpose, and fulfillment. This life defies the odds and transcends the limitations of previous generations.

## What Do YOU Want?

In the annals of exploration, few stories are as compelling as the race to be the first to reach the South Pole. It's a story of two explorers, Roald Amundsen, a Norwegian, and Robert Falcon Scott, a British naval officer, both locked in a fierce battle against nature—and each other—to claim a first in human history. The race to the South Pole remains one of the most striking tales of ambition, contrasting triumph and tragedy. Amundsen, with years of rigorous preparation under his belt, was driven by a pure passion for exploration. Scott, on the other hand, spurred by a sense of national pride, was determined to plant the British flag on the pole, despite being less seasoned in the polar extremes.

Amundsen, the seasoned explorer, was not just preparing for an expedition; he was crafting a masterstroke. His preparation was exhaustive and meticulous. He learned from the Inuit people about cold-weather survival, dog-sledding, and the wearing of animal skins in preference to the heavy, woolen parkas that could become damp and freeze. His team carried out extensive tests on food and equipment, ensuring they could withstand the grueling conditions. Every detail, from the type and number of sled dogs to the design of their skis, was considered and optimized for efficiency and survival.

In contrast, Scott's preparation, while earnest, lacked the same level of detail and adaptation to the polar environment. His team relied on motor sledges that broke down early in the journey, ponies that were ill-suited to the icy terrain, and heavy wool clothing that, while warm, offered little flexibility against the polar chill. His mission, fueled by a desire for national pride and personal glory, did not account for the punishing realities of the Antarctic as thoroughly as his competitor's.

As both teams embarked on their journeys, the differences in their approaches began to tell. Amundsen's team moved with precision, their well-practiced routines allowing them to cover ground efficiently. They built cairns (stone markers) to guide their return journey and stored caches of supplies strategically along their route. The Norwegian team reached the pole on December 14, 1911, a testament to their relentless focus and preparation.

Scott's team faced hardship after hardship. The mechanical sledges failed, the ponies succumbed to the cold, and the men found themselves man-hauling their supplies, which severely depleted their strength. They reached the pole on January 17, 1912, to the disheartening sight of the Norwegian flag. Their return journey was a battle against exhaustion, starvation, and extreme weather. In the end, the harsh Antarctic claimed the lives of Scott and his brave men, only 11 miles from a supply depot that could have offered them salvation.

This poignant chapter of exploration is more than a historical account; it is a profound lesson in the pursuit of dreams. Amundsen's success underscores the critical importance of not only a clear vision and meticulous strategy but also choosing the right goal. He didn't just identify a dream; he ensured it was a dream aligned with his skills, passion, and expertise. He then approached it with a step-by-step plan that meticulously accounted for every detail and possibility.

Conversely, Scott's tragic fate serves as a stark reminder of the consequences when ambition, however noble, is pursued without the necessary foresight and when the goal chosen is not entirely suited to one's capabilities and circumstances. His aim, while admirable, was perhaps more influenced by external expectations and prestige than by a true personal calling aligned with his abilities and experience.

As we reflect on these narratives, we see a mirror reflecting our own goals and aspirations. To truly succeed, we must not only plan with the thoroughness of Amundsen but also ensure that the goals we set are the right ones for us. It's about marrying our ambitions with a deep understanding of our strengths and limitations, passions, and practicalities. With a well-considered plan, unwavering determination, and the wisdom to choose goals that resonate with our true selves, we can overcome the formidable challenges that lie in our paths.

This lesson forms a foundational principle of "The Strangest Secret": the combination of the right mindset, a clear and suitable goal, and a detailed, well-thought-out plan makes us unstoppable. Let the stories of these polar explorers inspire you to embrace your challenges with confidence and clarity. Remember, the pursuit of a dream, no matter how challenging, is not just about reaching the destination; it's about embarking on a journey that's authentically yours, one that leads to triumph when pursued with intention, insight, and meticulous planning.

## The Power of Goal Setting

Earl Nightingale's timeless message in "The Strangest Secret" underscores a crucial truth: "We become what we think about." This principle highlights the transformative impact of positive thinking and underscores the critical need for setting precise, achievable goals. Without a clear and defined vision, it's all too easy to wander off course, becoming entangled in distractions that draw us away from our true objectives.

To bring this concept to life, consider the wise words of motivational speaker Zig Ziglar: "You can't hit a target you can't see." This simple yet profound idea captures the essence of goal setting. Identifying what a significant life means to you, and then crafting a distinct, actionable goal toward it, is essential. It's not just about having a goal but about having a goal that is vivid, detailed, and tangible.

This is where the Dreams List becomes an invaluable tool to help you clarify and articulate your aspirations. By using the Dreams List, you move from abstract dreaming into concrete goals, breaking down your larger vision into smaller, manageable steps, and making consistent progress toward your ultimate aim.

The Dreams List is your personal roadmap. It guides you as you navigate an exciting journey from where you are now to where you want to be.

In essence, the power of goal setting lies not just in the act of setting goals but in the process of carefully crafting and methodically pursuing them. With the Dreams List as your guide, you are equipped to take on this process, turning your dreams into a series of achievable steps. By committing to this approach, you align your daily actions with your long-term vision, paving the way toward a life of success, fulfillment, and purpose.

## You Are the Author of Your Own Story

As you embark on this journey of self-discovery and goal-setting, embrace the reality that you are the author of your own narrative. The choices you make today will script the chapters of your future. It's your moment to grasp the reins of your destiny and steer it toward a path lined with purpose, passion, and deep fulfillment.

This path is about actively shaping your life's story with each decision you make. As you navigate through your life, let your Dreams List be the guide that helps you plot, pursue, and ultimately achieve the life you aspire to. Think of each goal you write down as a milestone in your unique journey, a testament to your progress, and a marker of your success.

The act of writing down your goals daily is a ritual and a powerful tool that keeps your aspirations in clear sight, constantly reminding you of the direction you've chosen. This practice ensures that your goals stay at the forefront of your mind, fueling your actions and decisions each day. Remember, in the story of your life, each goal you set and work toward is a significant stride toward crafting a narrative of triumph and fulfillment that is uniquely yours.

## The Power of Written Goals

In a fascinating Harvard study, researchers discovered a significant difference in the success rates of individuals based on whether or not they set clear, written goals. The results revealed that those who took the time to write down their goals were forty-two percent more likely to achieve them than those who did not.

In my opinion, this forty-two percent should be one hundred percent. Without taking the time to sit down and identify what we're here to achieve, what we're working toward, and what we want, how are we supposed to achieve anything? Without identifying and carefully crafting our goals, we have nothing to aim for. This goes back to Ziglar's quote: 'You can't hit a target you can't see.'

So, while Harvard says that those who write down their goals are forty-two percent more likely to hit them, the first step is that you are one hundred percent more likely to hit goals you sit down and create. Writing down our goals and thinking about what we want forces us to clarify our thoughts, establish specific targets, and create a tangible roadmap for success.

## Committing to Success

When we commit our aspirations to paper, we take the first step toward making them a reality. This process provides us with a sense of purpose and direction and increases our motivation and commitment to the tasks at hand. As we progress through our journey toward living the life of our dreams, we must remember the tremendous value of setting clear, written goals. Doing so significantly increases our chances of success and empowers us to take control of our destinies.

## We Become Who We Surround Ourselves With

A massive part of becoming what we think about is controlling what we think about. The easiest way to do that is to control who is influencing us, and the easiest way to do that is by upgrading our circle of influence. The problem for most people is they need to act in ways that create a desire for successful people to be around them.

Daily, we are constantly influenced and conditioned by various factors, including the voices we hear. Recognizing the impact of these influences is crucial, especially when it comes to achieving success. Let's explore five critical tips for effective communication and personal development that can help expand our circle of influence and help us foster meaningful connections.

1. **Express Gratitude, Even For the Small Things:** One powerful way to expand our circle of influence is by replacing unnecessary apologies with expressions of gratitude. Rather than saying, "I'm sorry," shift your language to "Thank you." An example being when someone waits up for you to join them. This simple change allows you to convey appreciation and positivity in your interactions. By expressing gratitude, you uplift others and create a more conducive environment for building connections and fostering collaboration.

2. **Project Abundance Rather Than Neediness:** The words we choose shape our mindset and influence our interactions. To expand our circle of influence, reframing statements of need into expressions of preference or desire is essential. Instead of saying "I need," opt for phrases like "I'd prefer" or "I want." This conveys a sense of abundance and choice, projecting confidence and empowerment. Adopting this language shift invites opportunities and opens doors for meaningful connections.

3. **Sincere Acknowledgment Builds Trust and Rapport:** Acknowledging others' accomplishments sincerely is a powerful tool for expanding your circle of influence. When you genuinely recognize and appreciate the achievements of those around you, it builds trust and rapport and strengthens relationships. Take the time to offer specific compliments and praise for their efforts. Your authentic acknowledgment fosters a positive environment and encourages others to engage with you on a deeper level.

4. **Employ the Two-Second Rule for Thoughtful Responses:** Effective communication requires active listening and thoughtful responses. To avoid impulsive reactions, embrace the two-second rule. When someone speaks to you or presents an idea, briefly count to two in your head before responding. This pause lets you gather your thoughts, consider your words, and respond

clearly. By practicing this rule, you demonstrate respect for others' perspectives and enhance the quality of your interactions.

5. **Reflective Listening for Deeper Connections:** Building influence also means making others feel valued and understood. Practice reflective listening—summarize and echo back what the speaker has said. This demonstrates your engagement and understanding of their perspective. Making others feel heard lays the foundation of trust and paves the way for stronger, more meaningful connections.

By tuning into the voices and beliefs that shape your thoughts and actions daily, you take a proactive step toward broadening your influence. The strategies of expressing gratitude, projecting abundance, giving sincere acknowledgment, practicing the two-second rule, and actively listening to make others feel heard are not just communication tools. They are transformative practices that can deepen your connections, expand your reach, and enhance your opportunities for growth and success. Building meaningful relationships is an integral part of this journey, and each step you take on this path brings you closer to the realization of your goals. By upgrading the voices and conversations around you, you upgrade the thoughts in your own head.

As we move forward, the principles we've explored in this chapter lay a strong foundation for the power of goal-setting. Understanding and applying the concepts from "The Strangest Secret" to a Significant Life, we learn that our thoughts and actions are pivotal in shaping our destiny. The path to living the life we envision for ourselves is paved with the goals we set and the actions we take toward achieving them. This journey is not a sprint but a marathon, requiring persistence, adaptability, and a continuous focus on our desired outcomes.

## Embracing Lifestyle Design and the Ambition Habit

As we turn the page to the next chapter, we explore the dynamic concepts of lifestyle design and the ambition habit. This chapter will guide you through the process of intentionally crafting your life, and aligning it with your deepest values and priorities. Lifestyle design isn't just about setting goals; it's about creating a holistic approach to living that resonates with who you truly are and what you genuinely want. We will explore how embracing the ambition habit can transform your aspirations into reality, making your dreams an integral part of your daily life.

You'll discover how to harness these tools to build not just a list of dreams, but a life that truly reflects your aspirations and ambitions. With dedication, insight, and the right strategies, your journey toward a dream-filled life is just beginning.

# CHAPTER 5
# Lifestyle Design & The Ambition Habit

In a world where many simply coast through life on autopilot, the concept of lifestyle design shines brightly as a hopeful path for those seeking to infuse their existence with purpose and passion. At its core, lifestyle design is about deliberately crafting a life that reflects your true values and deepest desires. Alongside this, the ambition habit – the practice of relentlessly chasing your dreams – empowers you to break free from the constraints imposed by society or your own doubts. Together, these approaches offer a powerful way to start reshaping your life on your terms.

## Golden Standard of Ambition

Referring back to Elon Musk from earlier, his extraordinary life might seem like a rare exception, but it's a powerful example of what can be achieved with the right mix of ambition and strategic planning. As the CEO of trailblazing companies like Tesla, SpaceX, and X (formerly Twitter), and a key figure behind revolutionary endeavors like PayPal and OpenAI, Musk stands as a symbol of boundless ambition and relentless drive. His achievements didn't just appear magically; they are the fruits of a meticulously structured plan, guided by principles of lifestyle design and the ambition habit.

### Musk's Journey

From a young age, Musk was passionate about transforming the world and pushing the boundaries of human innovation. He targeted three major sectors for transformation: sustainable energy, space exploration, and artificial intelligence. Keeping these lofty goals in focus, Musk meticulously sculpted his life to turn these visions into reality.

His approach to lifestyle design was marked by a series of strategic choices. He opted to study at prestigious universities like Queen's University and the University of Pennsylvania, laying a solid educational foundation. His journey took a pivotal turn in Silicon Valley, where he first co-founded Zip2 and then established X.com, which later evolved into PayPal. Each step was a deliberate move toward his larger goals.

Musk's journey is a canvas of relentless pursuit and bold innovation. After the sale of PayPal, he could have comfortably retired, yet his vision stretched far beyond financial success. He plunged into sectors that were rife with challenges and skepticism. With SpaceX, he aimed to revolutionize space travel, a domain traditionally dominated by governmental giants. Musk's vision extended to Tesla, where he sought to spearhead the transition to electric vehicles in a market heavily reliant on fossil fuels. Each of these ventures was a leap into the unknown, driven by a desire to not just create businesses, but to initiate significant changes in the world.

This unyielding drive is the embodiment of the ambition habit. Musk didn't just dream; he committed every ounce of his being to bringing these dreams to life. His path was fraught with challenges. At one point, both Tesla and SpaceX were on the brink of failure. Musk faced a crucial decision–distribute his remaining funds between the two companies or focus on just one. He chose to split the funds, a risk that brought him to the edge of personal bankruptcy. This critical moment underlined his commitment to his ambitions, embodying the philosophy that the pursuit of significant dreams often involves substantial risks and challenges.

Musk's relentless ambition continues to drive him toward newer, groundbreaking endeavors. Currently, he is spearheading projects like Neuralink, Starlink, and The Boring Company, each unique in its vision and potential impact. Neuralink focuses on developing implantable brain-machine interfaces, with the ambitious goal of merging human consciousness with AI, potentially revolutionizing how we interact with technology and address neurological disorders. Starlink, meanwhile, aims to provide global internet coverage through a constellation of satellites, seeking to bridge the digital divide and bring connectivity to the most remote corners of the world. The Boring Company, with its focus on building low-cost, efficient underground transportation tunnels, reflects Musk's vision of solving urban traffic congestion and reimagining urban transit.

Each of these projects is united by a common thread: they're not just business ventures; they're Musk's attempts to address some of humanity's most pressing challenges and push the boundaries of what's possible, staying true to his lifelong habit of ambitious, transformative thinking.

## Dream Life = Design X Ambition

Musk has always been all about chasing his dreams, even when things got tough. His current projects aren't just about building more successful businesses; they're about solving big problems and thinking about the future in new ways. This go-getter attitude is at the heart of how Musk lives his life, always aiming high and not being afraid to take risks, no matter what people say about him or how he makes people feel. He's not afraid to bring *his* dreams to life no matter what anyone else says, which makes him polarizing, sure - but I also hope it's inspirational. You get one life, *your* one life.

As we move forward in our own lives, Musk's story can inspire us to be just as bold and focused. He once said, "When something is important enough, you do it even if the odds are not in your favor." This idea is perfect for lifestyle design and the ambition habit. It's about believing that our goals are worth going after, no matter what obstacles we might face.

# Examples of Intentional Lifestyle Design

Lifestyle design is a powerful tool for steering our lives toward success, especially when we consciously align our actions with our values and aspirations. While we've looked into Elon Musk's and other successful people's journeys of relentless ambition and innovation, another exemplary figure who has masterfully employed lifestyle design and who didn't come from wealth is Oprah Winfrey. Some, like myself, might argue that her success story is more relevant than the others *because* of the vast difference between her very meager beginnings and the unimaginable heights she's been able to take her career.

## Oprah Winfrey's Story: A Testament to Lifestyle Design

Oprah's life story is a remarkable testament to the power of intentional lifestyle design. Born into poverty in rural Mississippi and faced with numerous adversities from a young age, Oprah was determined not to let her challenging beginnings dictate her future. With a deep-seated passion for communication and a heartfelt desire to make a positive impact, she set her sights on a career in media.

Oprah's journey in the media world started in radio before moving to television, where she found her true calling. Her unique approach to talk shows, characterized by empathy, openness, and deep personal engagement, quickly set her apart. The launch of 'The Oprah Winfrey Show' marked a turning point, not just in her career but in the landscape of American television. The show became a platform for entertainment, but more importantly, for education, empowerment, and social change.

Beyond television, Oprah's aspirations saw her branching into various realms, including film production, publishing, and philanthropy. Each of these ventures was aligned with her larger vision of inspiring and supporting others. Her dedication to personal growth and her commitment to living a life that reflected her values turned Oprah into a global icon. She transformed her hardships into a powerful narrative of triumph, becoming a beacon of hope and resilience.

## From Humble Origins to Global Influence

The journey of Oprah Winfrey is a vivid example of how someone from a modest background can harness their passions and entrepreneurial spirit to build a global influence. Her story transcends the realms of media and entertainment, impacting areas like philanthropy and social advocacy. It's a powerful illustration that your beginnings don't define your potential for extraordinary success. With intentional lifestyle design, aligning your life with your core values and ambitions, you can achieve remarkable heights.

Icons like Musk and Oprah Winfrey each tapped into the power of lifestyle design to carve out extraordinary lives. Their achievements span various industries and interests, yet they share a common thread – a life driven by passion, purpose, and meticulous planning. These narratives serve as compelling evidence that with the right mindset and steadfast determination, anyone can craft a life that mirrors their deepest dreams and desires.

It might be tempting to dismiss these stories as unique, to think, "That could never be me." However, the essence of the Dreams List is to challenge and change that mindset. It reinforces the idea that anyone can achieve 'unicorn' status in their own right. It's about treating every step, not as a minor progression, but as a crucial, defining moment in a grander journey. Chip and Dan Heath's "The Power of Moments" emphasizes this concept beautifully, showing how stepping outside the norm can create defining, life-changing moments. Each decision, each action, can be a significant turning point, propelling us toward a life that is not only successful but also rich with meaning and impact.

## Breaking the Script:
## The Magic of the Ordinary

In our quest to design a life that reflects our deepest ambitions and values, let's explore the concept of 'breaking the script' through the story of the Magic Castle Hotel in Los Angeles. At first glance, this hotel doesn't stand out with extravagant architecture or luxury amenities. However, it has garnered an impressive reputation and a devoted clientele. The secret to its success lies in how it has masterfully 'broken the script' by offering unexpected and delightful experiences. Imagine calling a popsicle hotline and having treats delivered to you poolside, or enjoying a complimentary 'snack' menu at any time. These unique touches elevate an ordinary hotel stay into an extraordinary experience, creating memorable moments for guests.

Randy Pitchford, the Magic Castle's owner, was able to tap into the wants and needs of his hotel's guests and provide experiences beyond their wildest dreams. Referring back to our Empathy section in Chapter 1, we see that Pitchford, at some point, had the necessary paradigm shift between just wanting more money, to wanting his money to help others. Of course, both things can be true at the same time, which is what I'm here to help you do. Make your money to make your dreams come true... *and* make your dreams make you more money through the law of reciprocity.

## Incorporating the Power of Moments into Lifestyle Design

The Magic Castle Hotel's approach provides valuable insights into how we can apply the principles from "The Power of Moments" by Chip and Dan Heath in our journey of lifestyle design and cultivating the ambition habit. Here's how we can translate these ideas into our lives:

1. **Recognize the Routine:** Begin by identifying the everyday routines and norms that shape your life. Awareness of these patterns is the first step in pinpointing opportunities to create impactful and defining moments.

2. **Disrupt the Expected:** Once you're aware of your routines, challenge yourself to exceed expectations and add elements of surprise or joy. It could be something small like changing your morning routine or something bigger like spontaneously going on an adventure.

3. **Make it Memorable:** Aim to make the moments you create stand out. This could mean introducing contrasting experiences, heightening the element of surprise, or injecting a sense of novelty. The goal is to create experiences that are distinct and memorable.

4. **Stay Authentic:** In breaking the script, it's vital to stay true to who you are. Craft moments that resonate with your personal goals and reflect your true self. Authenticity ensures that these moments are not only unique but also meaningful to your journey.

By embracing these strategies, you can start to design your life with the same creativity and thoughtfulness as the Magic Castle Hotel. It's about transforming the mundane into the magnificent, and the everyday into the extraordinary. As you apply these lessons, each day becomes a canvas for crafting moments that not only surprise and delight but also align with your deepest aspirations and values.

## Elle Liu's Journey: Crafting a Dream Through Moments

In our pursuit of dreams, recognizing the power of moments and deliberately designing impactful experiences is crucial. This is evident in the inspiring story of Elle Liu, an entrepreneur with a vision for eco-friendly bedding. Faced with sleep-related issues, Elle researched and discovered the environmental downsides of the cotton industry. This realization was a defining moment for her, setting her on a new path.

Driven by her experience, Elle explored alternatives and found eucalyptus fabric as a sustainable solution. She then boldly invested in windmills, aligning her company's operations with her environmental values. This decision was more than a business move; it was a commitment to her dream of making a positive planetary impact.

Before starting Eucalypso, Elle achieved remarkable success, graduating from Princeton and working at American Express, Mastercard, and SoulCycle. The support she received from her network, particularly from her initially hesitant parents, was another defining moment. It validated her ambitions and reinforced her belief in her vision. This support, combined with her self-belief, helped Elle navigate the challenges of entrepreneurship.

Today, Eucalypso stands as a testament to Elle's success, transforming her sleep-related challenges into a thriving business. Her journey exemplifies the impact of intentionally creating defining moments and aligning actions with aspirations. Elle's experience serves as an inspiring reminder that with focus and determination, dreams can indeed become reality. It's often said that luck involves being at the right place at the right time. However, Elle's story suggests that many of us encounter these 'lucky' moments all the time but do not seize them due to unclear goals or unsuitable mental states. Recognizing and grabbing these opportunities is key to turning dreams into reality.

## Moments Turned to Habits

Our daily habits significantly influence our long-term achievements and overall happiness. Understanding the science of habit formation is key to creating lasting, positive changes in our lives, shaping both our identity and environment.

Charles Duhigg, in his book "The Power of Habit," explores the psychology and neuroscience behind habit formation, focusing on the 'Habit Loop,' which comprises a cue, routine, and reward. Recognizing these elements enables us to replace negative habits with beneficial ones, fostering healthier and more productive behaviors.

A cue triggers the habit, acting as a signal for the brain to initiate a behavior. The routine is the behavior itself – the habitual action we perform. Finally, the reward is what the brain gets out of the habit, reinforcing the loop and making it more likely that the behavior will be repeated. By identifying and understanding these components in our own lives, we can start to unravel and reshape our habits. Duhigg emphasizes that recognizing these elements in our negative habits allows us to replace them with more positive, beneficial ones. This understanding leads to the development of healthier and more productive behaviors, transforming our daily lives and ultimately our long-term success and happiness.

For instance, consider someone who has a habit of snacking on junk food while watching TV. The cue in this scenario is sitting down to watch TV. The routine is the act of snacking, and the reward is the enjoyment or comfort derived from the snack. By understanding this Habit Loop, one can change the routine while keeping the same cue and reward. Instead of reaching for junk food, they might choose a healthier snack or engage in a different activity like sipping tea. This small change in routine, while maintaining the familiar cue and reward, can lead to a healthier habit.

Building on this, James Clear's "Atomic Habits" emphasizes the impact of small, daily actions in shaping our lives. Clear's framework for changing habits involves four similar key steps:

1. **Cue**: Identify what triggers your current habit.

2. **Craving**: Understand what you crave from the habit and how it makes you feel.

3. **Response**: Change the behavior to a healthier or more productive one.

4. **Reward**: Find a reward that satisfies the craving but is aligned with your new, positive habit.

For example, if you habitually check social media (cue) for a sense of connection (craving), replace it with a call to a friend (response), fulfilling your need for connection in a more meaningful way (reward). This approach gradually builds new, beneficial habits that align with your goals and values.

The Harvard study on "The Happiness Advantage," led by Shawn Achor, offers insightful research into the power of positive habits. Achor, in over a decade at Harvard, conducted extensive studies involving thousands of executives worldwide, demonstrating how a positive mindset can significantly enhance performance and potential. His work reveals that adopting positive habits like gratitude, exercise, and meditation not only increases happiness but also leads to greater success and resilience across various life aspects.

This research underscores the critical role of positive habits in achieving well-being and professional success. The "Happiness Advantage" concept emphasizes that a happier, more positive mindset is not a result of success but the key driver of it. By incorporating habits that foster positivity, individuals can unlock higher levels of achievement and improve their overall quality of life. Achor's findings are a compelling reminder of the profound impact our daily habits and mindset have on our ability to excel in a world of increasing challenges and stress.

## Developing Positive Habits for Lifestyle Design

By developing positive habits and using them as guiding principles, we can create the life we want and achieve our goals. By intentionally cultivating habits that align with our values and aspirations, we not only improve our daily lives but also shape our identity and environment in a way that supports our pursuit of happiness and success.

By harnessing the power of habit formation, as described in the works of Duhigg, Clear, and Achor, we can make transformational changes in our lifestyles, ultimately leading to the creation of the life we truly desire.

## Identifying Goals and Building Supporting Habits

To transform our lives, we must first clearly identify our goals and dreams. This means understanding what truly matters to us, what we're passionate about, and what we want to achieve. Once these goals are defined, the next step is to determine the habits that can support these goals. For instance, if your goal is to become healthier, habits like regular exercise, mindful eating, and adequate sleep are foundational.

The process of building these supporting habits involves small, consistent steps. Start with manageable changes and gradually integrate them into your daily routine. For example, if your goal is to read more books, start with a few pages each day and gradually increase. Consistency is key; it's the small daily actions that accumulate into significant changes over time.

Remember, the journey toward your dreams is as important as the destination. Each step, each habit formed, is a building block in creating a life aligned with your passions and purpose. By intentionally developing habits that support your goals, you can create a sustainable path toward living a life that's both fulfilling and inspiring.

## Embracing Intentional Lifestyle Design

After identifying our goals and supporting them with the right habits, it's crucial to adopt the philosophy of intentional lifestyle design. It's about consciously shaping our lives to mirror our deepest values and aspirations. By proactively directing our actions, we establish a habit that fuels our ambition and determination, turning our daily activities into purposeful strides toward a fulfilling future.

Here's how to implement this approach:

1. **Define Clear Goals:** Clearly articulate your aspirations in various life aspects – for me, it's health, wealth, happiness, creativity, relationships, and work. Write them down explicitly. For me, I write down a goal in each area for each year from now until five years down the road

2. **Develop Supporting Habits:** Identify habits that will aid in achieving each goal. For example, habits for running a marathon would include daily exercise, healthy eating, and rest.

3. **Create Small, Achievable Steps:** Break habits into small, manageable actions. Start with something as simple as a daily run and gradually increase.

4. **Incorporate into Daily Routine:** Make these steps a regular part of your daily schedule to ensure consistency.

5. **Track and Reflect:** Monitor your progress with a journal or app, and adjust as needed. To me, this may be the most important step.

6. **Seek Inspiration and Get Into Bigger Rooms:** Learn from others who have successfully designed their lifestyles and developed ambition habits. Try to always be the "smallest person in the room." If you're the most fit, most successful, etc then you are in the wrong room.

7. **Commit to Continuous Improvement:** Regularly reevaluate and enhance your approach to lifestyle design and habit formation.

By embracing these steps, the ambition habit will become an integral part of your routine, aligning your daily actions with your long-term goals and values.

## The Ambition Habit Framework

The Ambition Habit Framework is a unique approach that merges the concepts of habits and lifestyle design, creating a powerful tool for achieving success. This method focuses on intentionally developing habits that align with our ambitions and aspirations. By doing so, we can effectively shape our environment to support these goals.

At its core, this framework believes that our daily habits, when aligned with our dreams and goals, become a formidable force driving us toward success. It involves identifying supportive habits and diligently integrating them into our routines, thereby crafting a life that truly reflects our deepest desires.

This approach not only asks us to evaluate our current habits and their effects on our lives but also encourages us to actively transform our surroundings. By making strategic changes to our environment, we create a space conducive to nurturing our ambitions and cultivating the necessary habits to achieve our goals.

The Ambition Habit Framework is dynamic and adaptable, empowering individuals to take charge of their lives and carve their paths to success. It's a holistic blueprint, combining habits, lifestyle design, and ambition to guide us in creating a life that resonates with our values, aspirations, and full potential.

## Research on the Ambition Habit

In their groundbreaking study "The Power of Intentional Change: A Model of Personal Growth," featured in the Journal of Personality and Social Psychology Review, Richard M. Ryan and Edward L. Deci explored the crucial role of intentional action in personal growth. Their research underscores that progress and development are the results of deliberate, positive habits and actions rather than mere chance or external factors. By focusing on intentional actions and forming positive habits, individuals can steer themselves toward sustained personal growth and achieve their desired goals.

Ryan and Deci's findings bolster the concept of the ambition habit in lifestyle design. It's not enough to simply wish for change; active and conscious habit formation is essential. This study highlights that our daily choices and habits significantly shape our life's trajectory. By intentionally cultivating habits that align with our aspirations, we can indeed create a life that not only achieves our goals but also reflects our deepest values and aspirations.

## The Ambition Habit in Action: Building Your Dreams List

By integrating intentional lifestyle design with the ambition habit, we set the stage for a deeply satisfying life that echoes our values and aspirations. This approach involves more than just goal setting; it's about crafting a life by nurturing habits and shaping our environment to reflect what truly matters to us, be it in our careers, personal relationships, health, or leisure pursuits.

As we transform ambition into a daily habit and use it as our guiding light, we meticulously design our lives to align with our aspirations, creating the life we desire. This process involves self-reflection, setting goals, and developing supporting habits. It's a dynamic journey, requiring us to constantly reassess and evolve our plans.

Now that you've gotten into the right mindset, started understanding your passions, tackled money beliefs, and learned to manage time, set goals, and why it's crucial to design your desired lifestyle, we're ready to move forward and unveil the Dreams List, transcending the typical bucket list. The Dreams List isn't just a collection of fleeting desires; it's about weaving a tapestry of goals that resonate with your soul, unlike the often superficial bucket list. This list marks the intersection of your ambition habit and lifestyle design, guiding you toward a future meticulously crafted from your deepest dreams. Brace yourself for a journey that challenges the conventional bucket list, turning the page to a new chapter where your aspirations are not just dreamed but lived.

# The Dreams List (What)

# CHAPTER 6
# The Dreams List vs. the Bucket List

I t's an all too familiar scene: sitting around with friends, discussing otherworldly travel destinations and wildest ambitions. Suddenly, someone likes an idea and says they're going to add it to their "bucket list," a collection of experiences and goals that one hopes to achieve before they, well, die.

It's a term that has become deeply ingrained in our culture. While it's often used lightheartedly, the underlying concept is rooted in a more somber reality—the inevitable march toward our mortality. But what if we were to flip the script? Instead of focusing on the list of accomplishments we hope to achieve before we pass on, why not embrace a more proactive, life-affirming approach to goal setting? Enter the Dreams List, an alternative to the traditional bucket list that encourages us to envision our ideal lives and pursue our passions with intention and purpose every day while we *are* still here.

## A Shift in Perspective

The Dreams List represents a dynamic shift from the traditional bucket list. Just as we discussed the Paradigm Shift in Chapter 1, this shift is not just about accomplishing a series of tasks; it's about embedding your deepest desires and aspirations into your life's fabric. This approach is grounded in intentionality and aligns your goals with your core values, fostering a lifestyle that's not only aspirational but deeply meaningful.

Rather than adhering to a finite set of experiences, the Dreams List encourages ongoing investment in pursuits that genuinely resonate with you. In this chapter, we'll explore how this visionary approach to goal setting differs fundamentally from the bucket list. We'll dive into real-life stories of individuals who have adopted this approach, witnessing the profound transformations it has brought to their lives. It's about crafting a life story that isn't just extraordinary in achievements but rich in personal fulfillment and growth.

### Inspiration From History: JFK's Moonshot Goal

In 1961, President John F. Kennedy's audacious declaration to land a man on the moon before the decade's end set in motion one of history's most inspirational journeys. This mission, more than just a historical milestone, serves as a powerful analogy for crafting your Dreams List. Kennedy's goal, amid the era's technological limitations, was a testament to the power of setting grand, seemingly unattainable dreams and mobilizing collective effort to turn them into reality.

The Apollo 11 mission's journey to the moon, witnessed by millions globally, was a cascade of meticulously planned and executed steps. From the flawless launch of the massive Saturn V rocket to the precise translunar insertion that negated the need for planned trajectory corrections, each action was a critical component of the mission. The journey included Neil Armstrong and Edwin "Buzz" Aldrin navigating the Eagle lunar module from the command module Columbia, changing its orbit, and initiating a powered descent amidst computer alarms that were overcome by NASA's prior simulations and Mission Control's guidance.

Armstrong's masterful piloting to avoid a rock-strewn crater, manually maneuvering the Eagle until a safe landing spot was found in the Sea of Tranquility, marked a moment of high drama and skill. On the lunar surface, the astronauts' activities, from setting up scientific devices to collect data on solar wind composition, laser beams for Earth-Moon distance, and seismometer readings, to gathering rock and soil samples, were all critical steps in this groundbreaking mission.

These steps in the Apollo mission resonate with the process of creating a Dreams List. It's about more than just envisioning an end goal; it's about recognizing and valuing each small, actionable step toward that goal. The moon landing demonstrates how each well-planned action, no matter how small, contributes to achieving something extraordinary. As you embark on creating your Dreams List, remember the Apollo mission's lessons: every step counts, meticulous planning is key, and even the most audacious dreams can be realized with persistence, ingenuity, and by leveraging other people. Just as the Apollo mission reached the moon, your Dreams List can guide you to achieve your life's most aspirational goals.

## The Bucket List

During my travels and conversations, I often come across people who claim to have a bucket list of things they wish to accomplish or experience before they die. However, when pressed for details, many of these people struggle to produce a tangible list, revealing that their so-called bucket list is more of a vague collection of wishes than a well-defined road map for living a life of purpose and passion.

The term "bucket list" can be traced back to the phrase "kick the bucket," which is an expression for dying. It was made popular in 2007 with the release of the film *The Bucket List*, which tells the story of a terminally ill man who embarks on a journey to fulfill his dreams before he dies.

While the concept of a bucket list can be powerful for inspiring us to contemplate our future and the things we want to accomplish before we die, we risk losing sight of the present moment and the countless opportunities for growth, connection, and fulfillment that exist right here, right now, in front of us. The key is to create harmony between dreaming big and living fully in the present.

## Reframing the Bucket List as a Dreams List

By reframing our bucket list as a Dreams List, we can shift our focus from things we want to do before we die to the experiences and goals that will enrich our lives right now. This subtle change in perspective can help us embrace the present moment while cultivating a sense of purpose and passion that will propel us toward our dreams. In doing so, we enrich our lives today and create a legacy of meaningful experiences.

# The Dreams List Concept

The Dreams List concept, inspired by Dane Espegard and Matthew Kelly with their respective books "The Dream Machine" and "The Dream Manager," offers a fresh and exciting approach to goal setting and personal development. Unlike traditional goal-setting techniques, which often focus on setting achievable, realistic objectives, the Dreams List encourages individuals to explore their wildest dreams and desires without limitation.

The beauty of the Dreams List lies in its inclusivity. It encompasses all dreams, from the grandest ambitions to the most superficial desires, whether it's a goal you wish to achieve, an event you want to experience, a milestone to reach, or even a long-lost relationship you hope to rekindle. The Dreams List welcomes every aspiration, big and small.

## Creating a Dreams List

Creating a Dreams List involves casting aside self-imposed limitations and letting your imagination run wild. To get started, jot down any dream that comes to mind, regardless of whether it seems attainable or far-fetched. The process of writing these dreams down can be an incredibly liberating experience, as it allows you to explore your desires without judgment or self-censorship.

**(write 10 "dreams" of yours below)**

1._____

2._____

3._____

4._____

5._____

6._____

7._____

8._____

9._____

10._____

As you continue to build your Dreams List, you'll find that your perspective on goal setting and personal development begins to shift. No longer confined by what seems achievable, you'll be empowered to dream big and push the boundaries of what you believe is possible. You may even surprise yourself by discovering new passions and aspirations that you never knew existed.

Think of five more BIG dreams. Dreams that feel "unattainable" to the current version of you… like buying your favorite sports team, moving to Italy, or becoming a champion bodybuilder.

**(write 5 "big dreams" of yours below)**

1._____

2._____

3._____

4._____

5._____

(for an entire Dreams List template, go to alexrfunk.com)

# Embracing the Power of Imagination

The Dreams List transcends traditional goal setting by encouraging you to harness the power of imagination and believe in unlimited potential. This approach to goal setting and personal development opens up a world of possibilities, guiding us toward a life that's extraordinary in every sense.

# Applying The Dreams List to Your Life

As Helen Keller once said,

> **"The only thing worse than being blind
> is having sight but no vision."**

It's time to start dreaming again and to make those dreams a reality.

## Maybe The Most Famous Dreamer

As a young man, Walt Disney's passion for drawing and art, developed in his early years, laid the foundation for his future endeavors. After a stint with the Red Cross army, Walt worked at the Pesemen-Rubin Art Studio in Kansas City, where he met

Ubbe Iwerks, a talented cartoonist. Together, they formed their company, but after facing initial challenges, Walt started Laugh-O-Grams, focusing on animated films.

In 1922, despite facing bankruptcy with Laugh-O-Grams, Walt's resilience shone through. He didn't give up; instead, he packed his unfinished print of 'The Alice Comedies' and headed to Hollywood to start anew. This determination led to the formal beginning of The Walt Disney Company in 1923.

Walt's breakthrough came with the creation of Mickey Mouse in 1928. This character, initially named Mortimer, was a product of necessity, marking a significant turning point for Disney's fortunes. The first film featuring Mickey with sound, a novel concept at the time, became an instant worldwide sensation, leading to a series of successful Mickey Mouse cartoons.

Following Mickey Mouse's success, Walt Disney continued to innovate. He introduced Technicolor to animation with the Silly Symphonies series, and 'Flowers and Trees,' part of this series, won him his first Academy Award in 1932. In 1934, defying skepticism, Walt embarked on producing the first animated feature-length film, 'Snow White and the Seven Dwarfs.' Despite being labeled as "Disney's Folly," the film premiered in 1937 to tremendous success, redefining the motion picture industry.

## Multiple Dreams

Walt Disney's dream of building a theme park was also initially met with skepticism and challenges. He envisioned a place where adults and children could enjoy rides and attractions together, a novel concept at the time. Despite facing doubts and financial hurdles, Disney persisted. He creatively financed Disneyland through a television deal with ABC and invested heavily in the project. Disneyland, opened in 1955 in Anaheim, California, was an instant success, attracting millions of visitors in its first few years.

The success of Disneyland led to the creation of Walt Disney World in Florida, which opened in 1971. Disney World expanded on the concept of Disneyland with additional theme parks, resorts, and attractions. Today, Disney's dozens of theme parks worldwide are a testament to his vision and determination, generating revenue that surpasses the initial investments and skepticism many times over, transforming the entertainment landscape and becoming beloved destinations for millions of visitors annually.

Walt Disney is a testament to the power of dreaming big and persistently working toward those dreams. His approach embodies his belief that courage is crucial in leadership, especially in pioneering new endeavors. His visionary spirit and adventurous approach to blazing new paths in entertainment have made a lasting impact, inspiring countless individuals to pursue their dreams with similar courage and determination.

## Building Your Dreams List

As we move to the next chapter, prepare to really start creating your Dreams List. This next step is where you transform your dreams (aspirations) into actual tangible plans.

Here, you don't need to worry about "work/life" balance and can start to see how your Dream Life all works together in harmony at the same time.

It's time to draft the blueprint for a life filled with excitement, meaning, and fulfillment.

The upcoming chapter is your starting point to dreaming without limits. Break free from the traditional all-encompassing bucket list and allow yourself to explore the vastness of your potential, one category at a time.

# CHAPTER 7

# The Categories of
# the Dreams List

As you create your Dreams List, it's essential to remember that breaking down your aspirations into smaller, more manageable categories can significantly affect your ability to achieve them. In this chapter, we will explore the nine main categories of the Dreams List, offering you a clear path and plan to guide your journey toward living the life of your dreams.

Imagine, if you will, a master chef preparing to create a delicate feast. Instead of simply tossing every ingredient into a pot and hoping for the best, the chef carefully selects each component, considering how they will harmoniously blend to create the perfect dish. Similarly, by categorizing our dreams and aspirations, we can craft a more focused and practical plan to bring them to fruition.

## Edmund Hillary Showing Us That Harmony Trumps Balance

Sir Edmund Hillary's life was a testament to the spirit of living our dreams. His most renowned achievement, the successful ascent of Mount Everest in 1953, alongside Tenzing Norgay, marked a pivotal moment in the history of mountaineering. This feat was not just a physical triumph but a symbol of pushing human limits and exploring the unknown. What most don't know is that Hillary's adventures extended beyond Everest, encompassing expeditions to the South Pole and the Himalayas, reflecting a life lived in relentless pursuit of discovery and challenge.

Hillary's ascent of Everest catapulted him into global fame, opening doors to numerous material opportunities. He leveraged his status to engage in various business ventures, pen books, and embark on lecture tours. He smartly used his earnings and reputation to fund additional expeditions, demonstrating a keen sense of financial acumen. His career in mountaineering allowed him to enjoy personal achievements, but he also leveraged those successes into financial stability and the ability to continue his passions.

Sir Edmund Hillary's life was deeply enriched by his family, as well. His wife, Louise Mary Rose, and their three children were central to his world. Hillary's dedication to his family illustrates the importance of maintaining strong personal relationships amidst a life filled with adventure and achievements. His ability to balance his passion for exploration with his role as a husband

and father showcases the harmonious blend of personal and professional fulfillment.

Health and physical fitness were paramount in Hillary's life as a mountaineer. He adhered to a strict training regimen to prepare for the rigors of his expeditions. This focus on health and well-being was a testament to his discipline and commitment to his goals. Hillary's attention to his physical fitness underscores the significance of health in achieving and sustaining success in demanding endeavors.

Hillary's success in mountaineering was as much a product of his skills and creativity as it was of his physical strength. His ascent of Mount Everest required innovative solutions to unforeseen challenges, demonstrating his ability to think creatively under pressure. Hillary's skillset extended beyond physical prowess; it encompassed a sharp, problem-solving mind that played a crucial role in his legendary achievements.

Though not overtly religious, Hillary found spiritual solace in the mountains and the natural world. His expeditions were more than just physical journeys; they were also spiritual quests. He possessed a profound reverence for the environment and the cultures he encountered, reflecting a deep spiritual connection with the world around him. Hillary's experiences in the mountains were as much about internal exploration as they were about external achievements.

Sir Edmund Hillary's legacy extends far beyond his mountaineering achievements. His life's purpose was deeply rooted in his commitment to philanthropy, particularly in Nepal. He established the Himalayan Trust, channeling his resources and energy into building schools, hospitals, and bridges for the Sherpa community, significantly enhancing their quality of life. This dedication to philanthropy underscores his belief in using personal success for the greater good, further proving that money doesn't have to be the root of all evil. His efforts demonstrate that a truly meaningful life is not measured solely by personal achievements and material gains, but is also defined by a profound commitment to positively impacting the lives of others, a legacy that continues to inspire through ongoing educational, health, and conservation initiatives.

As you start building your Dreams List, remember that the process is designed to be enlightening, not overwhelming. Sir Edmund Hillary was able to have the success he enjoyed because of a commitment to goals and values that were in harmony with one another. You'll be categorizing your dreams into nine distinct areas, but don't worry—I'll guide you through each step, ensuring that everything comes together cohesively in the later sections of the book.

This methodical approach will help you create a comprehensive and well-rounded vision for your future, encompassing all aspects of your life in a way that's both manageable and inspiring, just like Sir Edmund Hillary did.

| TRAVEL | ADVENTURE | MATERIAL |
|--------|-----------|----------|
| 455 | 264 | 149 |

As you continue on this journey, remember that the key to success lies in your ability to remain focused, adaptable, and open to the endless possibilities that await you. When crafting your Dreams List, it's helpful to divide our aspirations into nine main categories. Doing this can create a well-rounded vision for our lives that encompasses all aspects of personal fulfillment.

## 1. Travel

This category includes dreams about exploring the world, immersing ourselves in new cultures, and embarking on unforgettable journeys. Examples range from grand aspirations like visiting every continent and climbing Mount Everest to simpler joys such as taking a road trip through your own state.

## 2. Adventure

In this category, we focus on experiences that push our boundaries, such as skydiving, bungee jumping, or embarking on a safari. But adventure doesn't always have to be grand; it could be as simple as fulfilling a lifelong wish, like cooking Easter dinner with your grandma.

## 3. Material

This category encompasses dreams of acquiring material possessions that hold personal significance, from grand acquisitions like purchasing a dream home or owning a private island to smaller joys like getting a luxury watch or a piece of cherished artwork.

## 4. Career and Finance

This category captures aspirations of professional success and financial stability, including ambitious goals like starting your own business or achieving financial freedom, as well as smaller milestones like getting a promotion or saving for a special vacation.

## 5. Family and Relationships

In this category, we explore dreams connected to our relationships with others, such as getting married, starting a family, or mending a broken relationship. It can also include smaller, yet meaningful goals like planning a family reunion or creating a new tradition with loved ones.

## 6. Health

This category is about living a healthy lifestyle and achieving physical and mental well-being, from significant changes like losing weight or quitting smoking to smaller steps like starting a daily meditation practice or learning Aunt Suzie's cookie recipe.

## 7. Skills and Creativity

Here, we focus on dreams of mastering a skill or honing our creativity, such as learning to play an instrument, writing a book, or painting a masterpiece. It can also include smaller creative pursuits like taking a pottery class or starting a personal blog.

## 8. Spirituality and Faith

This category encompasses dreams related to spiritual growth and faith, including grand aspirations like going on a pilgrimage or studying with a spiritual teacher, as well as smaller acts like joining a local faith community or starting a daily prayer practice.

## 9. Legacy

Finally, this category includes dreams of lasting impact on the world, such as starting a scholarship or having a street named after you. It can also encompass smaller acts of kindness, like volunteering at a local shelter or mentoring a young person.

By dividing our Dreams List into these nine categories, we can better visualize and pursue our dreams, ultimately creating a life that aligns with our values and aspirations. This comprehensive approach ensures that we don't neglect any area of our lives.

# Unlocking the Potential of Categorizing Your Dreams

Psychologist and author Dr. Jordan Peterson offers valuable insight into the process of goal setting. In his words:

*"Breaking down your goals into smaller, more manageable categories is essential in achieving success. Focusing on specific areas of your life allows you to set achievable benchmarks and take meaningful steps toward achieving your dreams."*

## The Science Behind Categorizing Dreams

In line with Peterson's perspective, research by Szu-chi Huang at Stanford Graduate School of Business underscores the effectiveness of categorizing goals. Huang's comprehensive study involved different scenarios, all aimed at understanding how goal segmentation impacts achievement.

One aspect of her study involved students and their writing tasks. Those who initially worked with sub-goals wrote more than their peers with a single overarching goal. This finding suggests that breaking down larger aspirations, like our diverse dream categories, into tangible steps can significantly enhance initial progress and commitment.

The study also included a collaboration with a crowdsourced marketing company, further exploring this concept in a real-world context. Workers tasked with uploading book information from local bookstores were divided into three groups, each employing a different goal-setting approach.

One group was assigned an overarching goal of earning eighty points over eight days. The second group was given a series of eight smaller sub-goals, each worth ten points, to be achieved daily. The third group followed a hybrid approach: they worked toward ten-point sub-goals for the first four days and then shifted their focus to the overall eighty-point goal for the remainder of the project.

The results were clear. The group given only the overall goal uploaded information on 1,268 books. The group with the sub-goals uploaded information on 1,392 books. However, the hybrid group, which combined both strategies, significantly outperformed the others, uploading information on 1,906 books. Not only did this group upload the most information, but a higher percentage of its members achieved the eighty-point target. The daily activity patterns also revealed interesting insights. The hybrid group's productivity declined gradually in the first half but then surged in the latter half as they shifted focus to the larger goal.

This study's findings are a testament to the power of combining short-term milestones with a long-term vision. The hybrid approach, balancing the immediate satisfaction of achieving sub-goals with the motivation drawn from an overarching aim, proved to be a potent formula for sustained effort and successful outcomes. Such an approach, as incorporated into the Dreams List, when applied to our personal dreams and aspirations, can similarly enhance our journey toward achieving them.

## Information Chunking

These findings reinforce the idea of "chunking" information, a cognitive strategy that involves breaking down complex news into smaller, more digestible pieces. When we apply the same principle to our goals, we can overcome obstacles more efficiently and steadily progress toward our dreams.

Individuals could identify and tackle the steps necessary to achieve their goals by focusing on specific categories. Imagine, for a moment, that you're an aspiring artist who dreams of exhibiting your work in a prestigious gallery. Instead of being overwhelmed, you could break it down into smaller goals:

- Honing your artistic skills (dream to add and cross off: take art class)

- Building a portfolio (dream: launch website for my art)

- Networking with other artists and gallery owners (dream: join art mastermind)

- Promoting your work (dream: sell first painting)

These smaller goals can be further divided into smaller tasks, making the path to your ultimate dream clearer and much more achievable.

Suppose you dream of running a marathon. This big goal can feel daunting at first. To make it more manageable, you could break it down into smaller goals:

- Start with regular short runs to build stamina. (dream: run/walk one mile)

- Gradually increase your running distance each week. (dream: run one whole mile without stopping)

- Participate in smaller races, like 5Ks or 10Ks, to gain experience. (dream: run a 5k)

- Focus on nutrition and recovery to maintain physical health. (dream: pay a running coach)

- Set a target for the marathon and train specifically toward that distance. (dream: follow a marathon training plan for 20 weeks)

If your dream is to start a small business, say, a café, you could divide this large goal into smaller, actionable steps:

- Conduct market research to understand customer needs and preferences. (dream: watch a YouTube video on how to do market research)

- Develop a business plan outlining your vision, budget, and strategy. (dream: learn how to make a business plan)

- Secure funding, either through savings, loans, or investors. (dream: learn how to get funding from an investor)

- Find the perfect location for your café. (dream: find a commercial realtor to partner with)

- Lock in the location and space for the café. (dream: sign lease for first cafe)

- Purchase equipment and hire staff. (dream: open café to public)

In both scenarios, the overarching dream is broken down into smaller, achievable goals, each a step toward the final aspiration. This approach makes the journey less overwhelming and more structured, increasing the chances of success.

This further emphasizes the importance of breaking dreams into smaller, more manageable categories, providing a solid foundation for your Dreams List.

## Embracing the Categories of Our Dreams List

These categories remind us of the importance of connection, the thrill of exploration, and the value of shared moments with loved ones. In my journey of working toward my Dreams List, I've discovered the significance of each category in shaping the course of my life.

The **Travel, Adventure,** and **Family and Relationships** categories have been instrumental in planning fun and exciting experiences that create lasting magic moments and memories. On the other hand, the **Material** and **Career and Finances** categories have played a crucial role in setting benchmarks and rewards for myself. After selecting and achieving the goal of saving up for a down payment on a house, I experienced a sense of accomplishment and financial stability that boosted my overall well-being. Similarly, focusing on career aspirations such as earning a promotion led me to concentrate on skill development and improved work performance.

The **Health, Skills and Creativity,** and **Spirituality and Faith** categories are profoundly personal and have allowed me to set meaningful goals for self-improvement. Training for a marathon and learning a new language have taught me discipline, pushed my limits, and increased my self-confidence. These categories represent the journey of self-discovery and personal growth, reminding us to always strive for our best selves.

Lastly, the **Legacy** category serves as my compass, guiding how I show up daily and pushing me to work toward who I aspire to become.

| LEGACY |
| --- |
| 122 |
| thank 100 soldiers |
| thanks a soldier every time i see them |
| beat elliot james at SOMETHING cutco rel |
| always have thank you cards on me (to gi |
| become incorprated |
| be featured on 5 podcasts in general |
| Have "meet alex funk" on someone elses |
| get verified on IG |
| Positively impact 1,000 people |
| 10,000 |
| 100,000 |

I'm driven to leave a positive impact on the world through volunteer work, mentoring, and how I show up for the people around me. This awareness helps me remain conscious of my actions and words. I consistently strive to become a better version of myself, show up for those around me in the version of myself I wish to become, and leave the legacy that I want to leave behind.

As we journey through this book, my aim is to actively involve you in the process through sharing my experiences and insights. The next step? Let's start applying these dream categories to your life.

On the following pages, you'll find blank spaces labeled 1-3 under each category. I encourage you to pause here and list your top three dreams in each category. Don't worry, I've provided examples to spark your imagination and get you started. This exercise is a crucial part of creating your Dreams List and turning abstract aspirations into concrete goals. By actively engaging in this task, you are taking your first steps toward a life that's not only dreamt about but actively pursued.

## TRAVEL

1. _____

2. _____

3. _____

## ADVENTURE

1. _____

2. _____

3. _____

## MATERIAL

1. _____

2. _____

3. _____

## CAREER/FINANCES

1. _____

2. _____

3. _____

## FAMILY/RELATIONSHIPS

1. _____

2. _____

3. _____

## HEALTH

1. _____

2. _____

3. _____

## SKILLS/CREATIVITY

1. _____

2. _____

3. _____

**SPIRITUALITY/FAITH**

1. _____

2. _____

3. _____

**LEGACY**

1. _____

2. _____

3. _____

# Join Us in the Journey of Pursuing Dreams

As we move forward, we will begin turning the dreams you've just listed into your new reality. We'll explore how to deconstruct each dream into smaller, manageable steps, making them more attainable. This process will empower you to set clear benchmarks and take meaningful actions toward realizing your dreams. Together, we'll navigate the complexities of dream-chasing, equipping you with the tools and strategies needed to bring your aspirations to life. So, let's embark on this exciting journey, step by step, to live the life you've always dreamed of.

# CHAPTER 8
# The Different Types of Dreams and How to Pursue Them

Lawrence R. Samuel's fascinating exploration, "The American Dream: A Cultural History" takes us on a journey through the American Dream's evolution from its humble beginnings in the colonial era to the intricate tapestry it represents today. With a keen sense of storytelling, Samuel unveils a gradual transformation of the American Dream from its initial straightforward desire for land ownership and economic prosperity to its current multifaceted embodiment of social mobility, equality, and freedom. Whether or not you're American and no matter how you feel about the American Dream, Samuel's work gives us a lot to dissect when it comes to what people are "dreaming" about and why they usually fail to accomplish these things.

# The Different Types of Dreams

As we dive into this captivating narrative of the American Dream, we discover that the dreams people chase are as diverse as the individuals pursuing them. They can range from:

- **Material Dreams**: fueled by the longing for a better life by acquiring tangible possessions.

- **Social Dreams**: driven by the aspiration for social recognition, belonging, and acceptance.

- **Political Dreams**: encompassing the hope for a fair and just society that upholds the principles of democracy and the common good.

## Pursuing Our Dreams Effectively

So, what does this mean for our Dreams List? How do we go about pursuing them effectively? To begin, it's essential to recognize that our dreams, like the American Dream, are dynamic and multifaceted, reflecting the complex nature of human desire and aspiration.

## Material Dreams

For those chasing material dreams, the key is to strike a balance between ambition and contentment. Setting realistic, achievable dreams for acquiring the material possessions we desire while considering the intangible values that contribute to a fulfilling life is essential. We must remind ourselves that material possessions, though gratifying, are not the sole measure of our worth or happiness. It's also important to be honest with yourself in this section. If your goal of owning a big house has more to do with sticking it to your middle school bully and less with needing that much space, you could be ticking off the wrong goal.

## Social Dreams

Building genuine connections and nurturing a sense of community is paramount in pursuing social dreams. By fostering relationships based on trust, empathy, and mutual respect, we not only elevate our social standing but also contribute to the well-being of others, creating a more inclusive and compassionate society.

## Political Dreams

When it comes to political dreams, active engagement, empathy, and advocacy are essential. Educating ourselves on the issues that matter, participating in civil discourse, and supporting initiatives aligning with our values allows us to become agents of change and drive progress toward a more equitable and just world.

Pursuing our dreams effectively requires a nuanced understanding of the different types of dreams and a tailored approach to achieving them. As you reflect on the diverse categories we explored in the previous chapter, apply that framework to acknowledge the intricate nature of your aspirations. This process will guide your purposeful steps toward realizing them, moving you closer to living the life of your dreams, one dream at a time. Again, consider the captivating story of the Apollo 11 mission, where a remarkable interplay of different types of dreams—grand, shared, and simple—contributed to the awe-inspiring achievement of landing on the moon and returning safely to Earth. Each aspect of this monumental feat can be traced back to specific dream categories, offering a clear example of how varied dreams, when pursued with intention and clarity, can lead to extraordinary outcomes.

## Runway Dreams: Foresight and Planning

Like NASA's long-term goals and benchmarks for the Apollo 11 mission, runway dreams require foresight and careful planning. The ambitious objective of landing on the moon and returning to Earth demanded a clear vision, meticulous preparation, and the unwavering commitment of all involved. As we explore the realm of runway dreams, we are reminded of the importance of setting ambitious goals and working tirelessly toward their realization.

Runway dreams are akin to a plane taking off: they need a long runway before they can soar. These dreams often start as distant aspirations, requiring extensive groundwork and patience. Unlike instant gratifications, they unfold over time, necessitating continuous effort and resilience. This type of dream benefits from detailed roadmaps, outlining each step of the journey. Breaking down a runway dream into smaller objectives can make it less daunting and more manageable, allowing for adjustments and refinements along the way. It's about embracing the process, and understanding that the path to achieving these dreams is often as significant as the dream itself.

For example, imagine aspiring to become a renowned chef. This runway dream starts with basic culinary training, followed by years of honing skills in various kitchens. Each stage, from mastering knife skills to understanding flavor profiles, further paves your runway. Gaining experience, building a reputation, and perhaps even traveling the world to learn different cuisines are all part of the preparation. Finally, opening a successful restaurant or earning prestigious awards becomes achievable. This dream requires talent, but moreso, strategic planning, perseverance, and a passion for continual learning and growth.

## Chance Dreams: Embracing the Unexpected

Even the most meticulously planned endeavors are not immune to the unexpected, as illustrated by the chance dreams that emerged during the mission. The Eagle lunar module's computer alarm during the landing is a stark reminder that unforeseen events can arise anytime, demanding adaptability and resourcefulness. Embracing chance dreams requires us to acknowledge life's unpredictable nature and develop the skills to adapt and thrive in uncertainty.

Chance dreams are those serendipitous moments that, while unplanned, can lead to remarkable outcomes. They thrive on spontaneity and open-mindedness, often requiring a quick pivot or a leap of faith. Unlike runway dreams, chance dreams do not follow a structured path; they emerge from being in the right place at the right time and having the courage to seize the opportunity.

For instance, consider a musician casually performing in a local bar, only to be discovered by a talent scout. This chance dream didn't stem from meticulous planning but from being open to opportunities and ready to showcase talent at any moment. Perhaps playing at that local bar x- number of times per month is the smaller dream this musician was working toward on this chance encounter. The musician's dream of a successful career takes a significant leap forward, propelled by a mix of preparedness and fortune.

Chance dreams often materialize from the most ordinary moments, transforming them into extraordinary opportunities. Picture yourself attending a casual networking event and unexpectedly meeting the CEO of your dream company, leading to your dream job. Or, imagine going to a garage sale and finding a hidden masterpiece, a chance purchase that turns into a fortune. Envision discovering a hidden talent for pottery in a random class, opening up new avenues for creativity and career. And think of the thrill of unexpectedly meeting a sports icon like Tom Brady, a moment of awe and inspiration.

A dream will rarely happen to be walking past your couch when you need it most.

## Manifestation is Real

These dreams, emerging from serendipitous encounters and nurtured by our reticular activating system's ability to recognize opportunities, underscore the importance of remaining receptive to the myriad of possibilities that life presents us each day.

The reticular activating system (RAS) is a network of neurons located in the brainstem that plays a crucial role in regulating wakefulness and sleep-wake transitions. It acts as a filter for the massive amount of information processed by our brains, helping to focus our attention on certain stimuli while ignoring others. Essentially, the RAS helps determine what is brought to our conscious attention.

When it comes to goal setting and achieving dreams, the RAS can be influential. By consistently focusing on specific goals or dreams, we can essentially 'train' our RAS to identify resources, opportunities, and information aligned with these objectives. This process makes it more likely for us to notice and seize opportunities that we might otherwise overlook, aiding significantly in the pursuit of our goals.

## Simple Dreams: The Foundation of Success

Amidst the grandeur of the Apollo 11 mission, we must not overlook the small wins that were essential to its success. These wins, such as the training of the crew and the assembly of the spacecraft, may appear mundane compared to the dazzling spectacle of a lunar landing. Yet, they form the very foundation upon which monumental achievements are built. By valuing and diligently pursuing our simple dreams, we lay the groundwork for realizing our loftiest inspirations.

Simple dreams are those small, achievable desires that bring joy and satisfaction to our daily lives. They are often overlooked, yet they play a significant role in enhancing our overall well-being.

These dreams don't require elaborate plans or major life changes; instead, they're about appreciating and achieving the little things that make life fulfilling. Whether it's baking a homemade cheesecake perfectly, replacing an old key fob with a new one that works seamlessly, or enjoying an evening at a comedy club, these simple dreams add a sense of accomplishment and happiness to our lives. They remind us to cherish the small victories and pleasures, building a foundation of contentment and gratitude.

For example, imagine setting a goal to create a small garden in your backyard. This simple dream involves selecting your favorite plants, dedicating time to nurture them, and enjoying the process of watching them grow. The satisfaction derived from this simple act of cultivating life in your own space is immeasurable. It's a reminder that, sometimes, the simplest dreams can be the most rewarding, grounding us in the present and adding a layer of richness to our daily experience.

Below, write out your five favorite dreams that you've brainstormed so far and circle whether each is a runway, chance, or simple dream.

**FIVE FAVORITE DREAMS**

1. _____

        Runway     Chance     Simple

2. _____

        Runway     Chance     Simple

3. _____

       Runway     Chance     Simple

4. _____

       Runway     Chance     Simple

5. _____

       Runway     Chance     Simple

## Creating a Roadmap to Success

Now that you've categorized a handful of your dreams as runway, chance, or simple, let's focus on creating a roadmap to success. This clarity in categorizing your dreams is a crucial step toward achieving them. Whether they are grand visions or everyday joys, understanding their nature allows you to approach them with the right mindset and strategy.

The Apollo 11 mission, a blend of all three types of dreams, exemplifies the power of this approach. Reflecting on this historic feat, we see how diverse dreams, when pursued with intention and collaboration, can lead to extraordinary achievements. Use these insights to navigate your own journey, embracing the unique characteristics of each dream to build a life filled with achievement and fulfillment.

As you embark on your journey, aligning your diverse dreams into a cohesive plan is crucial. This chapter helped you categorize your dreams, each distinct in its approach. However, as we go deeper, you'll discover how these seemingly separate dreams are, in fact, interconnected. Planning and pursuing one category of dreams often leads to unexpected progress in another.

Much like the Apollo 11 mission, where various types of dreams interplayed seamlessly, your own endeavors will likely reflect a similar synergy. This interconnectedness, coupled with qualities like teamwork, leadership, and adaptability, not only enhances your pursuit of individual dreams, but also contributes to the broader tapestry of your aspirations. By applying these lessons to your life, you'll find that, as you actively work toward one dream, you might 'accidentally' achieve others, creating a fulfilling journey that mirrors the spirit and success of Apollo 11.

## Strive for a Life Aligned With Our True Potential

The pursuit of dreams is a multifaceted journey offering tremendous potential for our lives and those around us.

As Marianne Williamson, author of "A Return to Love" insightfully noted, true passion stems from striving for a life that reflects our highest capabilities, not from settling for less.

Marianne Williamson said:

> *Our deepest fear is not that we are inadequate;*
> *our deepest fear is that we are powerful beyond measure.*
> *It is our light, not our darkness, that most frightens us. We*
> *ask ourselves, who am I to be brilliant, gorgeous, talented,*
> *fabulous? Actually, who are you not to be? You are a child of*

*God. Your playing small does not serve the world.*
*There is nothing enlightened about shrinking so that other*
*people won't feel insecure around you. We are all meant to*
*shine as children do. It's not just in some of us, it's in everyone.*

*As we let our own light shine, we unconsciously give other*
*people permission to do the same.*
*As we are liberated from our own fear, our presence*
*automatically liberates others.*

Pursuing the entirety of our dreams embodies Williamson's powerful message. By embracing the full spectrum of our aspirations, we step into our true potential, shining brightly in our unique capacities. This pursuit is not just about personal fulfillment; it's an act of empowerment, encouraging others to follow suit. As Williamson suggests, by liberating ourselves from fear and embracing our power, we not only realize our own potential but also inspire and enable those around us to do the same.

## Turning Dreams Into Goals

After recognizing the unique characteristics of each type of dream, we can organize and then prioritize our dreams, and we can start working toward them one at a time. Transforming a Dreams List into categories and dream types allows us to turn dreams into goals. Goals are much easier to break down because we can create tangible steps. There are many ways to pursue goals; one of the easiest methods is the SMART method.

## The SMART Method

A SMART goal is something very clear:

- **S**pecific: Target a particular area for improvement.

- **M**easurable: Quantify or suggest a progress metric.

- **A**chievable: Ensure you can achieve your goal with the given resources.

- **R**ealistic: Outline what results you can feasibly achieve using the available resources.

- **T**imely: Highlight when the goals should be achieved.

The SMART method of setting goals fits perfectly into what we're doing with chunking up our Dreams List into many smaller, actionable steps.

I take a similar approach by pushing my dreams planning even one step further. There are five different categories that I slot my dreams into on my Dreams List after identifying what *type* of dream they are (runway, chance, or simple):

1. **Right Now Goals:** These are dreams that I'm accomplishing within the next month.

2. **Up Next:** These are dreams that I'm completing or pursuing between one and three months from now.

3. **This Year:** These are dreams that I'm pursuing within three to twelve months.

**4. Future Focus:** These are dreams that I can follow and accomplish within one to three years from now.

**5. Distant Dreams:** These are dreams that I can see happening in the next three to five years. Most runway dreams end up here, while the steps involved in getting there end up slotted above.

By categorizing and prioritizing your dreams, you can effectively start working toward them.

Below, carry over your five favorite dreams and circle whether each is a right now, next up, this year, future focus, or distant dream.

## FIVE FAVORITE DREAMS

1. _____

    Now    Next    This Year    Future    Distance

2. _____

    Now    Next    This Year    Future    Distance

3. _____

    Now    Next    This Year    Future    Distance

4. _____

    Now    Next    This Year    Future    Distance

5. _____

Now    Next    This Year    Future    Distance

## Pursuing Your Dreams

Now that you've categorized your dreams, the journey to achieving them begins. In the upcoming chapter, I'll show you a variety of practical tools and techniques specifically tailored to help you cross off a ton of dreams. These resources are designed to help you organize your Dreams List, and to empower you with strategies for breaking down each dream into manageable, actionable steps.

We'll focus on how to effectively prioritize, track your progress, and adapt as needed, ensuring that you are equipped to tackle each dream with confidence and have some secret tools to help you get there.

# CHAPTER 9
## Tools for Your Dreams List

**M**y first encounter with Dane Espegard, a figure of unparalleled success and wisdom in the world of dream realization, came during my scrappy college years. Dane may now be known for his impactful consulting work with large companies centered around "dreaming" and being the "dreams guy" on many podcasts, but to me Dane will always be my first mentor and the person who taught *me* to dream.

As a student, I observed Dane in various settings - at conferences, in office meetings, leadership academies, and on exotic trips. I noticed that Dane almost always had a constant companion: a classic Jim Rohn journal. The understanding that Dane's journal is far more than a mere accessory has become a guiding principle for me. I believe his journal is the bedrock of his success, instrumental in shaping his achievements in so many areas of life.

I envision his journey coming to life within the pages of his past journals, each of which started with a blank sheet that turned into his strategic visions and aspirations. Witnessing Dane, the 'dreams guy,' regularly consult his journal reinforces my understanding of the profound impact that the right tools, like a journal, can have in the pursuit of dreams. It's this consistent practice, the ritual of translating thoughts into written words in a specific notebook, that highlights for me how such seemingly simple tools are, in reality, powerful allies in charting a course toward realizing one's dreams.

## Tools for Dreaming

Drawing inspiration from Dane Espegard's use of a journal, this chapter explores various tools that can act as catalysts in organizing, planning, and actualizing your dreams.

## A Notebook

A notebook, like the one Dane uses, is invaluable for jotting down your dreams and goals. Writing them out not only solidifies these aspirations in your mind but also makes them feel more tangible and achievable. You can use different sections for various types of dreams, track your progress, and reflect on your journey.

## Vision Board

A vision board offers a vivid and creative way to visually map out your dreams. By compiling images, inspirational quotes, and symbols that resonate with your aspirations, you create a tangible, motivating representation of your goals. Regularly seeing your vision board can keep your dreams alive in your daily consciousness.

## Digital Apps

In today's digital age, numerous apps are available to help organize your Dreams List. These apps often feature goal-setting frameworks, deadline reminders, and progress trackers. They can be particularly useful for setting milestones, receiving motivation, and keeping your aspirations organized and accessible.

## Accountability Partners

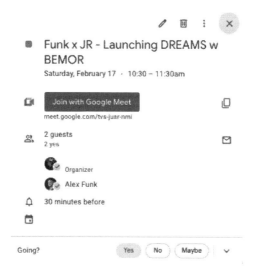

Pairing with an accountability partner who shares similar aspirations can greatly enhance your journey. Regular meetings to discuss progress, face challenges, and celebrate successes can keep you both motivated and on track, providing mutual support and encouragement. For me, the past few years have been laced with partners and friends that help keep me on track for my dreams.

## Meditation and Visualization Techniques

Incorporating meditation and visualization into your routine can powerfully support your dream pursuit. By mentally rehearsing your goals and visualizing success, you strengthen your belief in your capabilities. This practice can keep you focused and align your subconscious mind with your conscious efforts.

## Goal-Setting Workshops and Seminars

Engaging in goal-setting workshops or seminars offers structured guidance and expert strategies in dream planning. These sessions provide a supportive community and valuable insights into effective goal-setting and achievement techniques.

## Inspirational Books and Podcasts

Inspirational books and podcasts can provide a steady stream of motivation and practical advice. Listening to the stories of others who have achieved their dreams can spark ideas and offer different perspectives on tackling your own goals.

## Harnessing Tools for Monumental Achievements

By leveraging these tools and integrating them into your daily routine, you will be better equipped to make consistent progress toward your dreams, edging ever closer to the life you aspire to live. The significance of using the right tools is not just a concept in personal development but also a proven element in historical achievements. Reflect on pivotal moments like the Apollo 11 mission or Roald Amundsen's journey to the South Pole. These monumental events in history highlight how essential tools and equipment were not only for success but also for survival.

Picture the vast expanse of space—the seemingly infinite void that the astronauts on Apollo 11 had to traverse to reach the moon. This remarkable mission relied heavily on the lunar module, a spacecraft specifically designed to transport two astronauts from the lunar orbit to the moon's surface and back again. The Lunar Roving Vehicle (LRV), an electronic-powered vehicle, allowed astronauts to traverse the moon's surface more efficiently and cover greater distances. The iconic spacesuits were crucial for protecting astronauts from the harsh lunar environment, providing life support, and enabling communication.

Now, let's shift our focus to the tundra of Antarctica, where Roald Amundsen and his team embarked on their perilous journey to the South Pole that we discussed in Chapter 4. Ski equipment allowed Amundsen and his team to glide swiftly across the icy terrain, while dog sleds were pivotal in transporting supplies. Tents provided much-needed shelter against the harsh Antarctic elements, and carefully planned food supplies were crucial for their nourishment and survival. Similarly, warm clothing was essential to protect against the extreme cold.

These two extraordinary feats of human achievement underscore the indispensable role of tools in conquering seemingly impossible challenges. In the same way that specialized equipment was vital for the astronauts of Apollo 11 and Amundsen's team, everyday tools can be just as crucial in your journey toward achieving your dreams. Whether it's a fitness tracker for your health goals, a budgeting app for financial dreams, a language learning software for your educational aspirations, or even a simple planner to keep your daily tasks aligned with your long-term objectives, the right tools can simplify your path, keep you motivated, and assist in overcoming the hurdles you encounter. By thoughtfully choosing and utilizing these tools, you, too, can navigate the complexities of your Dreams List, transforming your aspirations into tangible realities.

## Tracking My Dreams

As you navigate your dreams journey, discovering a tracking and organizing method that resonates with you is vital. Your journey is unique, and so should be your approach to tracking your dreams. Think of this as an invitation to explore and find what works best for you.

Initially, I began with a rudimentary approach: a simple list on a paper sheet displayed above my desk. As my aspirations grew, so did my method and organization. I transitioned to a journal, a dedicated space for my dreams that I would consult periodically. It was a notebook, just a spiral thirty-cent Walmart notebook.

### Transition to Digital

I then moved my Dreams List from a notebook to the Notes app on my phone, which was also on my computer. This allowed for greater accessibility and convenience, as I would refer to my Dreams List often, if not every week. Pinning the note at the top of my app kept it even more within my sight. Every time I opened the Notes app, I saw "Dreams List" in big, bold letters, which reminded me to review my list every so often.

As my phone software evolved and widgets were added, it was even easier to add my Dreams List as a widget on my home screen. Now, every time I opened my phone, the words "Dreams List" were big and bold on my home screen, which reminded me to click on it, scroll through, and find a dream I could pursue right now. This was all before I had my dreams broken down, so just having all the dreams right there kept them at the top of my mind. At the time, I had 100-200 dreams.

## A More Comprehensive System

After attending my fourth Dreams Workshop from Dane Espegard, I was inspired to create a more comprehensive strategy. I designed a Google Word document, split into categories, which I used for about a year. Until a mentor, Nik, inspired me to turn the doc into a Google spreadsheet, which has now turned into a dreams database, housing all 2,000 of my current dreams on my list. What started as a kid scraping up money to attend a conference where a dreams workshop happened to be included, has evolved into a multifaceted system designed to take the guesswork out of helping you achieve your dreams while you're still alive to enjoy them.

## The Multifaceted Approach

This latest database, which I always have open in my browser, includes my master Dreams List. The first tab is a comprehensive list of 2,000+ life dreams, organized by category and color-coded according to dream type. The second tab is Completed Dreams, where I chronicle completed dreams from 2019 through 2024, the years between creating my first Dreams List and publishing this book. I update the entire workbook weekly when I do my weekly planning.

The third tab is my Dreams Planning tab. This is where I sit down, semi-annually, and plan out all the dreams I will pursue within those six months. I check in with the Dreams Planning tab regularly throughout the year to ensure that my next three months align with where I thought I'd be the last time I checked in.

The last tab is called Scattered Thoughts and Dreams. It is a space for inspiration, containing various ideas and dreams that I often revisit and add to my master Dreams List from there.

### An Even Easier Approach

Now, Dane has created an app that works just like my own personal database for you to house your dreams called the Dreams Vault. The app makes it easy to add your dreams and choose which ones you're currently working on or towards. I helped Dane tweak the software by referencing my own Dreams spreadsheet database in the creation process. To try the Dreams Vault, go to www.thedreamsvault.com/the-dreams-list-book.

# The Significance of the Right Tools

## A Chart of Achieved Dreams and Tools Used

Here, I include a chart that shows how many dreams I achieved throughout the years and what tools I was using during that time:

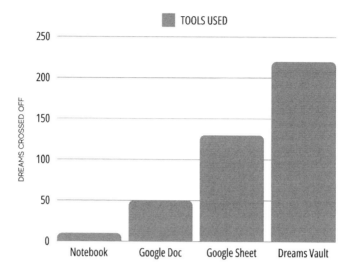

Remember, just as the Apollo 11 astronauts and Roald Amundsen needed specific tools for their monumental missions, you, also, require the right resources to turn your dreams into reality. The historic expeditions to the moon and the South Pole were successful not just because of the courage and skill of those involved, but also due to the meticulous selection and use of essential tools. This principle applies directly to your journey of dream realization.

As you embark on this path, consider how effectively using tools can significantly enhance your ability to achieve your dreams. My own experience has shown that the right tools–like a carefully organized database for tracking dreams, a dedicated space for scattered thoughts and ideas, and regular check-ins for planning–can transform lofty aspirations into achievable goals. By incorporating similar tools into your life, whether it's a digital planner, a vision board, or a simple notebook, you'll find that your dreams become more tangible and within reach. The key is to select tools that resonate with your style and needs.

## Learning from Blake Mycoskie

The journey of Blake Mycoskie and his creation of TOMS Shoes is a powerful example of leveraging modern tools to turn a vision into reality. Mycoskie's innovative use of the internet and social media was pivotal in transforming TOMS from a simple idea into a globally recognized brand. He effectively used these platforms to promote the unique one-for-one model of TOMS, where each purchase of a shoe led to the donation of a pair to children in need. This message resonated deeply with customers worldwide, largely due to the expansive reach and connective power of social media.

But Mycoskie didn't stop there; he also harnessed e-commerce platforms, allowing TOMS Shoes to sell and ship globally. This approach broadened his market exponentially, reaching customers far beyond traditional brick-and-mortar limitations. Furthermore, he utilized virtual meetings and video conferences to forge and maintain relationships with partners and donors across the world, a strategy that proved invaluable in expanding the brand's impact and reach.

Mycoskie's story illustrates the profound impact of correctly identifying and using modern tools in your dream pursuit. His success with TOMS Shoes demonstrates that with creativity, strategic planning, and the effective use of digital platforms, you can amplify your message, connect with a global audience, and realize your dreams, just as he did. Let Mycoskie's journey be a source of inspiration and a guide on how to harness the power of technology in bringing your own aspirations to life.

## Let's Go Live Your Dreams

As we've seen through the inspiring examples of the Apollo 11 mission, Roald Amundsen's South Pole expedition, and Blake Mycoskie's TOMS Shoes, the right tools are indispensable in turning ambitious dreams into reality. This chapter has introduced a range of tools, from simple notebooks to advanced digital platforms, emphasizing their role in making even the most challenging dreams achievable. But remember, it's not just about having these tools; it's about how you use them that truly matters.

As we turn the page to the next phase of your journey, our focus will shift from identifying tools to applying them within the framework of time management. The upcoming chapter is dedicated to executive-level time planning, a critical strategy to enhance your dream pursuit. We'll dive into effective time prioritization, crafting actionable daily, monthly, and yearly plans, and breaking down your goals into manageable tasks. These time management skills are crucial for maximizing the potential of your chosen tools, ensuring that each step you take is deliberate and impactful.

By honing these skills, you position yourself not just as a dreamer, but as a doer. Ready to embark on this next crucial phase? Let's step into a world where time is not a barrier, but a gateway to realizing your dreams.

# SECTION 3

# Achieving Your Dreams (How)

# CHAPTER 10
# Executive-Level Time Planning

Having already overcome the misconception in Chapter 3 that we don't "have time" for our dreams, it's now time to take it a step further. Time, invaluable and irreplaceable, demands our respect. Remember, it's more valuable than the money people often prioritize in their lives.

In this chapter, our journey takes a pivotal turn: from recognizing that we have enough time to learning how to masterfully manage it. We'll dive into executive-level time planning, a crucial skill that turns each moment into an opportunity to inch closer to our dreams. Here, it's not just about managing time—it's about strategically using it to our advantage, making sure every minute plays a significant role in the extraordinary life we aspire to lead.

# Picture Yourself as the CEO of Your Life

In a world where every second counts, you are responsible for making decisions that affect the direction of your aspirations. It's a weighty responsibility, but it can be harnessed to drive you toward success. Through the lens of executive-level time planning, we will examine how the great leaders and visionaries of our time manage their days to achieve remarkable results. We will observe how they prioritize their tasks, delegate responsibilities, and optimize their schedules to ensure each day is seized to its fullest potential.

We'll dive straight into practical time management strategies, showing you how to integrate these techniques into your daily life. This isn't just theory; it's about crafting a personal blueprint for action that fits seamlessly into your routine.

## Unlocking the Secrets of Top-Performing Executives

In a world where distractions abound, effectively managing time has become a highly sought-after skill.

A study conducted by the "Harvard Business Review" sought to uncover the secrets behind the success of top-performing executives. They discovered a powerful link between exceptional time management skills and outstanding performance. This doesn't sound too surprising, right? The study found that these high-performing executives possessed the remarkable ability to set priorities, delegate tasks, and steer clear of distractions. In contrast to their lower-performing counterparts, they were masters of their schedule, efficiently allocating their time to maximize productivity.

The study's authors pointed out that effective time management was not an innate talent but a skill that could be honed and refined. This revelation is both encouraging and empowering. By emulating the time management strategies of these successful executives, we, too, can elevate our performance and inch closer to realizing our dreams.

## Key Takeaways from Top-Performing Executives

### 1. Clearly Define Their Priorities

Top executives are masters at prioritizing. They know that not everything can be a top priority, so they focus on what truly matters. Start by listing all your tasks and dreams. Then, rank them based on their impact and urgency. Ask yourself, "Which of these will bring me closer to my dreams?" Focus on these tasks first. Remember, prioritizing is about making hard choices and sometimes saying no to good opportunities to say yes to great ones.

### 2. Delegate Tasks to Optimize Their Workload

Delegation is a key tool in an executive's arsenal. It's about understanding that you don't have to do everything yourself. Identify tasks that can be handled by others and delegate them. This could mean outsourcing, automating, or asking for help from friends or family. Delegating frees up your time for tasks that only you can do and that align closely with your priorities and dreams.

### 3. Unwavering Focus in the Face of Distractions

In a world brimming with distractions, maintaining focus is crucial. Executives often use techniques like time-blocking, where they allocate specific blocks of time to work on their priorities without interruptions. They also limit distractions by turning off notifications, setting clear boundaries, and practicing mindfulness. To emulate this, create a distraction-free environment when working on your goals. Prioritize tasks daily and dedicate time to them without multitasking.

## Integrating Executive Practices into Daily Life

These strategies aren't just for the boardroom; they can be life-changing when applied to personal goals and dreams. By adopting these practices, you can manage your time more effectively, giving you the clarity and focus needed to bring your dreams to fruition.

# Mastering Time Management: Techniques and Strategies

Mastery of our daily, weekly, and yearly schedule lies at the heart of effective time management. To do so, we must learn the art of planning for each day, week, month, semester, quarter, and year. This holistic approach to planning ensures we have a clear vision of the road ahead and a strong foundation upon which we can build our dreams.

One crucial technique to optimize our time usage is time blocking. This method involves dedicating specific blocks of time to particular tasks, allowing us to focus intently on the task at hand and minimize distractions. By assigning dedicated time for each job, we can work more efficiently and make meaningful progress toward our goals.

Of course, our plans and schedules are only as effective as our ability to evaluate and adapt them. Regular check-ins on how our time is spent are essential to ensure we use our most valuable currency wisely. By treating time as a precious resource, we can prioritize our goals and allocate our time accordingly.

## Lessons from Chet Holmes

In his book, The Ultimate Sales Machine, Chet Holmes emphasizes the pivotal role of time management in achieving business success. He argues that for salespeople, time is their most valuable asset, and managing it effectively is key to hitting sales targets and advancing their careers. Drawing inspiration from Holmes's insights, let's explore how you can apply these principles to all areas of your life, not just in sales.

### 1. Crafting a Well-Thought-Out Weekly Schedule

The first step to mastering your time is to create a structured weekly schedule. This isn't just about jotting down appointments; it's about strategically planning your week. Start by identifying your key goals for the week. These could be related to personal development, career advancement, or even leisure activities. Allocate specific times for these activities, ensuring a balance between work and personal life. Remember, a well-planned schedule should be flexible enough to accommodate unexpected events while keeping you on track toward your dreams.

## 2. Prioritizing Tasks Based on Significance and Immediacy

Holmes's approach to prioritizing tasks is crucial for effective time management. Apply this by categorizing your tasks into four quadrants: urgent and important, important but not urgent, urgent but not important, and neither urgent nor important. Focus primarily on tasks that are both urgent and important. Learn to recognize tasks that seem urgent but may not significantly impact your goals. This method helps in making informed decisions about where to allocate your time and energy.

## 3. Setting Clear Goals and Breaking Them Down

Setting clear goals is the cornerstone of effective time management. However, large goals can be overwhelming. Chet also talks about breaking them down into smaller, achievable tasks. For instance, if your goal is to write a book, start by setting a daily word count target. If you aim to run a marathon, begin with shorter, consistent training sessions. We've talked in depth about this concept already.

By creating a disciplined schedule, prioritizing tasks effectively, and breaking down goals, you can enhance your productivity and inch closer to achieving your dreams. Whether it's advancing in your career, nurturing relationships, or pursuing personal interests, mastering time management is a critical skill that can transform your aspirations into reality.

## My Weekly Time Management Routine

Mastering time management is about making intentional decisions on how we spend our time, aligning our actions with our goals and values. Here are my strategies for taking charge of my weekly schedule and enhancing productivity.

1. ***Centralized Calendar and Schedule:*** The first step toward effective time management is having a designated place to record and track commitments and tasks. Choose a system that works best for you, whether it's a physical planner, a digital calendar, or a productivity app. By centralizing your calendar, you create a reliable and easily accessible repository for all your obligations. For me, it's using Google calendar.

2. ***Weekly Mapping:*** The Sunday Ritual: Block out some time every Sunday night to map out your upcoming week. Any day of the week will work, but, in my opinion, Sunday is the best as it's the "first day of the week". Review existing commitments, including recurring meetings, classes, and personal activities. This comprehensive overview lets you identify available time slots and plan tasks accordingly. You set the foundation

for efficient time management by proactively scheduling your week ahead.

3. ***Define and Prioritize My Goals:*** To effectively manage your time, it's essential to identify and prioritize your goals. Consider the various areas of your life, such as relationships, fitness, work, and personal projects, and determine what truly matters to you. By consciously selecting priorities each week, you ensure that your efforts align with your values and aspirations.

4. ***Prioritization Within Priorities:*** Once you've established your priorities, it's crucial to prioritize specific tasks and activities within each category. Assess the urgency, importance, and potential impact of each task. Allocate your time based on these considerations, focusing on high-priority items aligning with your goals. This approach ensures you dedicate sufficient time and energy to tasks that truly matter. For me, a cheat code has been understanding the power of procrastination. For example, I have a running list of "Airplane Tasks" on my Notes app. This allows me to put off tasks that don't require internet, phone service, or a deadline, and enables me to be productive even while on flights with no internet. I have similar running lists for situations like "back home," "when a sales call cancels/no-shows," and "next month/year/decade". Next level time management is managing priorities and using procrastination to your advantage.

**5.** *Flexibility and Adaptability:* Unforeseen events or new tasks may arise during the week, threatening to disrupt your planned schedule. In such situations, it's vital to reassess priorities and make conscious choices about adjusting your schedule. Evaluate the significance of new tasks and determine how they fit within your existing priorities. Be open to rescheduling or delegating tasks when necessary, and recognize that specific tasks can be safely postponed without significant consequences. You can navigate unexpected challenges while staying focused on your goals by maintaining flexibility and adaptability.

These practices will help you do more than simply manage tasks; they're steps toward personal and professional fulfillment. Embrace these time management techniques to actively progress toward your Dream Life, starting today.

## Learning from Benjamin Franklin

Renowned author and speaker Jim Rohn always said that time is more valuable than money. Bearing this wisdom in mind, we will dive into the significance of time management by examining the life of one of America's Founding Fathers, Benjamin Franklin.

Franklin's strict daily schedule maximized his productivity, and he realized his goals remarkably. By allocating his time to specific blocks dedicated to various tasks, such as exercise, reading, writing, business, socializing, leisure, and self-improvement, he ensured that every aspect of his life received the necessary attention.

Franklin's commitment to optimizing his time usage involved reviewing and adjusting his schedule as needed, allowing him to accomplish more in a day than many could in a week.

This disciplined approach to time management contributed to his numerous achievements and inventions, such as creating bifocals, the lightning rod, the Franklin stove, and the flexible urinary catheter. In addition to his inventive prowess, Franklin was a successful businessman, politician, and one of the most influential writers of his era. His diplomatic skills and contributions to drafting the U.S. Constitution and Declaration of Independence further solidified his place in history.

Ben Franklin's life demonstrates the transformative power of effective time management, a lesson you can directly apply to your own dream pursuit. By adopting Franklin's discipline in organizing your daily and weekly schedule, you too can enhance your productivity and edge closer to achieving your dreams. Emulating his approach to time management offers a practical pathway to unlock your full potential. By managing your time wisely, every day becomes an opportunity to make significant progress in realizing your aspirations and bringing your Dreams List to life.

Seriously consider, how much more could you be doing with *your* life if you just simply took your time more seriously and not for granted? This, the way you are living right now, is your one life.

In this chapter, we've harnessed a few key time management strategies. Now, as we turn the page, we'll shift our focus to mastering another critical aspect: energy management. Just as time management is essential for achieving your dreams, so, too, is harnessing and optimizing your energy. In the next chapter, we'll explore how to manage and maximize your energy, ensuring you have the vitality and endurance to chase and live your Dream Life to its fullest.

# CHAPTER 11
# Having the Energy To Do It All

Pursuing our Dream Life demands a balance of mental and physical energy. In this chapter, we dive into both maintaining and enhancing your energy levels to help you manage the demands of your goals effectively.

## Physical Energy:

Our physical well-being plays a critical role in our overall energy levels. Studies highlight the benefits of connecting with nature and regular exercise in boosting energy. Incorporating outdoor activities and consistent physical exercise into our daily routine is beneficial for our health, and vital for sustaining the energy needed to pursue our dreams. Additionally, staying hydrated and maintaining organized spaces contributes significantly to our physical energy and ability to stay active and focused.

## Mental Energy:

Mental resilience and clarity are equally important. Research from the Harvard Business Review indicates a link between well-being and productivity. Practices like gratitude enhance our mental energy and alertness. It's about nurturing a mindset that supports our goals. Acknowledging the positives in our lives boosts our energy and resilience, especially during challenging times.

As we explore these aspects, we'll discover practical ways to harness both physical and mental energy, ensuring you're equipped to chase down your dreams with vigor and enthusiasm.

# Energy is the single most important key to success.

This profound truth was a significant takeaway from Tony Robbins (as discussed with his priming technique in Chapter 1), who emphasizes the concept of "Proximity is power." It's about who you surround yourself with, as it shapes who you become. But it's not just proximity; several factors cultivate your energy. At Tony's events, it's not just what he says but the energy he exudes that draws people in. Every interaction is an exchange of energy – be it giving through smiles, attentive listening, and encouragement, or taking. Social anxiety often stems from the fear of not being enough, but remember, people recall the energy you bring, not just your words.

And what is the catch-all for all of your energy in life? Environment. Your surroundings directly influence your energy levels, underscoring that environment equals energy.

As we dive into the ten categories of energy in the following section, keep in mind how each aspect contributes to and is shaped by the *environment* of them around you.

## Ten Categories of Energy

### 1. People:

The people in our lives have a profound impact on our energy levels. It's crucial to assess the influence of those around us, as we often align with the expectations of our peer group. Surrounding yourself with positive and supportive individuals can significantly boost your energy and motivation. It's often said that we are the sum of the five people we spend the most time with. Or that we rise and fall to the expectations of our peer group. Think of your social circle as a garden; nurture relationships that uplift you and prune those that drain your energy. By consciously choosing who you spend time with, you can create an environment conducive to growth and high energy. This choice can lead to an improved sense of well-being and a more energized approach to pursuing your dreams.

> ◆ *Raising Your Energy*: Imagine being part of a group that regularly engages in positive activities like group workouts or brainstorming sessions for personal projects. The collective enthusiasm and

support can be infectious, boosting your energy and inspiration. Such interactions often leave you feeling more motivated and capable of tackling your goals.

◆ *Draining Your Energy:* Conversely, spending time with people who constantly criticize or belittle your ambitions can be draining. If you're regularly exposed to negativity or pessimism, it can sap your energy and enthusiasm, making it harder to stay focused and optimistic about your dreams.

Rate yourself 1-10 on the **PEOPLE** you're surrounded by: _____ of 10

## 2. Fun:

Having more fun in different areas of life, whether at work, during social interactions, or in team meetings, can significantly boost energy levels. Incorporating enjoyable activities and playfulness into our daily routines can transform our well-being. Success shouldn't suck. Life shouldn't suck.

◆ *Raising Your Energy:* Imagine integrating playful elements into a regular workday or incorporating fun team-building exercises into meetings. These activities can transform the atmosphere, sparking creativity and enthusiasm, which in turn can make you feel more energized and engaged.

◆ *Draining Your Energy:* Conversely, a lack of fun and enjoyment can lead to a decrease in energy. Monotonous routines and all-work-no-play environments can contribute to burnout and a dip in your overall energy levels.

Rate yourself 1-10 on how much *FUN* you're having: _____ of 10

3. **Confidence/Self-talk:** Confidence is not just a feeling; it's a catalyst for energetic and successful interactions, especially in customer relations where assertiveness and self-assurance are key. Cultivating confidence involves practicing positive self-talk, which can significantly elevate your energy levels.

   ◆ *Raising Your Energy:* When you engage in affirming self-dialogue, you reinforce your self-worth and capabilities, which naturally increases your confidence. This heightened self-belief can translate into more dynamic and enthusiastic interactions, whether in sales, presentations, or daily communications.

   ◆ *Draining Your Energy:* Negative self-talk, on the other hand, can quickly erode confidence, leading to decreased energy and a hesitancy to face challenges.

Rate yourself 1-10 on your *SELF-TALK* lately: _____ of 10

4. **Stress:** Effectively managing stress is essential for maintaining optimal energy levels. Breathing exercises, tactile stimulation, and other stress management techniques can be used to manage stress. Adopting these practices can reduce the negative impact of stress and replenish our energy.

   ◆ *Raising Your Energy*: Techniques like focused breathing exercises can center your mind and reduce anxiety. Tactile stimulation, such as the use of stress balls or hand massages, can also be a quick, effective method to release stress and boost your energy.

   ◆ *Draining Your Energy*: Unmanaged stress can be a significant energy drain, leading to both physical and mental exhaustion.

Rate yourself 1-10 on your ***STRESS LEVELS*** lately: _____ of 10

5. **Phone Usage:** Our relationship with our phones can significantly affect our energy levels. Take some time to evaluate your phone usage habits. Being mindful of the content we consume and setting boundaries with our devices can help prevent energy-draining distractions and promote a healthier balance.

   ◆ *Raising Your Energy:* Mindfully managing phone time can enhance our focus and presence. For instance, dedicating specific times for checking emails or social media allows us to engage more deeply in other activities without constant interruptions. Something I have done is turned off every "badge" notfication on my phone so I see zero red circles and have also turned off almost all notifications to my lock screen, especially text messages and social media.

◆ *Draining Your Energy*: Conversely, excessive or undisciplined phone usage can lead to distraction and energy drain. The habit of constantly scrolling through social media or being available 24/7 can lead to fatigue and reduce our productivity.

Rate yourself 1-10 on your *PHONE* usage lately: _____ of 10

6. **Sleep:** Quality sleep is an essential pillar for maintaining high energy levels. It's the time when your body and mind recover and regenerate, preparing you for the challenges ahead.

   ◆ *Raising Your Energy:* Prioritize your sleep by establishing a regular bedtime routine and creating a sleep-conducive environment. This could mean investing in a comfortable mattress, using blackout curtains, or engaging in relaxing activities before bed.

   ◆ *Draining Your Energy:* Lack of sleep or poor sleep quality can significantly impede your energy. It leads to fatigue, reduces your ability to concentrate, and can negatively impact your mood.

Rate yourself 1-10 on your *SLEEP* lately: _____ of 10

7. **Food:** The impact of nutrition on energy levels cannot be overstated. Fueling our bodies with nutritious foods provides the necessary energy for optimal functioning. Incorporating a balanced diet, avoiding excessive sugar and processed foods, and staying hydrated is vital for sustaining high energy levels throughout the day.

   ◆ *Raising Your Energy*: Adopting a balanced diet filled with whole foods provides the nutrients needed for sustained vigor. Opt for foods rich in vitamins, minerals, and other essential nutrients that contribute to a steady supply of energy.

   ◆ *Draining Your Energy*: Conversely, diets high in processed foods and excessive sugar can lead to energy spikes and crashes, leaving you lethargic and unproductive.

Rate yourself 1-10 on the *FOOD* you're putting in your body lately: _____ of 10

8. **Fitness:** Physical activity and movement are vital in maintaining energy levels. Finding enjoyable ways to stay active through regular exercise, walking, or engaging in recreational activities can increase stamina, improve mood, and enhance overall energy.

   ◆ *Raising Your Energy*: Finding an activity you enjoy ensures that staying active isn't a chore but a refreshing part of your day. Whether it's yoga, cycling, or a dance class, enjoyable fitness not only enhances your physical well-being but also injects a burst of energy into all aspects of your life.

◆ *Draining Your Energy*: A sedentary lifestyle, on the other hand, can lead to sluggishness and decreased motivation. Trips to Europe show me how overweight and sluggish Americans are, and I have to believe the "drive everywhere" and "office job" lifestyles play a part in that.

Rate yourself 1-10 on how well you've been moving your BODY: _____ of 10

9. **Vision/History**: Reflecting on past accomplishments can be a powerful energy source. Acknowledging our achievements, both big and small, boosts self-confidence and motivation. Taking the time to appreciate our progress fuels us with positive energy and propels us forward. Just as powerful is our focus on our vision. This refers back to Chapter 4 and "The Strangest Secret." Now that you have your Dreams List, you can wake up every day with somewhere to go.

◆ *Raising Your Energy*: Celebrate your milestones, both large and small. This recognition nurtures self-confidence and renews motivation, providing a surge of positive energy to tackle future endeavors. With vision, write your goals down every day. Make a vision board. Meditate and visualize your goals.

♦ *Draining Your Energy*: Without a clear vision or sense of direction, your energy may scatter, leading to feelings of being lost or aimless. This lack of focus can drain your energy as you spend time on tasks that don't align with your ultimate objectives, leaving you exhausted and unfulfilled. Just as a ship without a compass wanders aimlessly at sea, a person without a clear vision expends energy without making true progress toward an exciting life.

Rate yourself 1-10 on your **VISION** for yourself: _____ of 10

10. **Gratitude:** Expressing gratitude increases energy and overall well-being. Taking moments to appreciate the people, experiences, and blessings in our lives cultivates a positive mindset. It infuses us with a renewed sense of energy and contentment.

♦ *Raising Your Energy*: Acknowledge the goodness in your life, whether it's the support of loved ones, achievements, or the simple joys of life. This practice can fill you with a powerful, positive charge, uplifting your spirits and energizing your pursuits.

◆ *Draining Your Energy*: Focusing on lacks or dwelling on negatives can sap your vitality. Gratitude flips this script, refocusing on abundance and success, which in turn replenishes your energy reserves.

Rate yourself 1-10 on how **GRATEFUL** you've been lately: ____ of 10

By actively managing our energy across these ten categories, we set ourselves up for a vibrant and dynamic life. Positive influences, joy in the everyday, effective stress management, physical health, and an attitude of gratitude—each play a part in boosting our energy. This, in turn, equips us to achieve our dreams with greater ease and vitality.

Now that our potential is unlocked, we can use the supporting routines that the Dreams List offers to implement them and continually improve each category. You'll notice, if you track this (once a week or once a month, etc), that the categories needing your attention won't always be the same. Where your focus goes, energy flows. So, it's important to be constantly evaluating and figuring out where you may not be showing up as the best version of yourself.

## Harnessing the Intangible: Tesla's Insight on Energy

The renowned inventor and scientist Nikola Tesla once remarked, "The day science begins to study non-physical phenomena, it will make more progress in one decade than in all previous centuries of its existence." This insightful statement highlights the potential for groundbreaking discoveries and advancement when science shifts its focus toward exploring the intangible aspects of our world.

By diving into the non-physical realm, like how to create more energy within us, we can unlock new possibilities and deepen our understanding of the universe, human nature, and the interconnectedness of all things. Tesla's words serve as an inspiring reminder that our quest for knowledge should be boundless and encompass all facets of existence, including those that may lie beyond our current comprehension.

Nikola Tesla's remarkable life is an excellent example of the importance of energy awareness and management.

A brilliant inventor and scientist, Tesla significantly contributed to electricity and energy. Despite his relentless work ethic, he accomplished much in his lifetime outside of work, primarily because of his skillful personal energy management. Tesla maintained a habit of taking regular daily breaks to rest, meditate, and recharge his mental and physical batteries. He also adhered to strict sleep, exercise, and diet routines, ensuring that he remained in optimal physical and psychological condition. Moreover, Tesla employed visualization techniques to generate new ideas and solutions more efficiently. He was ahead of his time in most of these things.

Learning from Nikola Tesla's mastery of energy, let's apply this discipline to our own energy management. You can utilize this focused awareness to elevate your life, making every moment count toward fulfilling your dreams. Embrace Tesla's principle: managing your personal energy with intention is a fundamental step toward success in any endeavor.

In this chapter, we've harnessed the essence of energy management, learning how to amplify our vitality to chase our dreams. We explored techniques to surround ourselves with positive influences, indulge in fun, handle stress, and nourish our bodies and minds. Now, we turn to Chapter 12, where we'll uncover the secrets to breaking bad habits and cultivating a success-oriented environment. It's here that we'll delve into establishing routines that make dreaming not just possible, but a natural extension of our daily lives.

# CHAPTER 12
## The Power of Habits, Routines, and Environments

Habits and routines are the quiet powerhouses behind our dreams. They shape our days and, ultimately, our lives. In this chapter, we dive into how these daily practices and the environments we craft can propel us toward our dreams, making them an effortless part of our reality. Take a moment to imagine the power of these influences quietly steering you toward or away from your dreams at this current moment.

Close your eyes for each and think about your:

◆ Daily habits

◆ Hourly habits

◆ Morning routines

◆ Afternoon routines

◆ Evening routines

◆ Daily environment

◆ Circle of influence

◆ Weekday environment

◆ Weekend environment

Starting with the people you're talking to, the people you surround yourself with, the voices you hear, the things you see on TV, and the things you see on your phone. What is your physical environment like? How clean is your car? (At that, what kind of car?) How comfortable and relaxing is the bedroom? How organized is the kitchen?

Routines and habits: what does your morning look like? What does your weekend look like? Take some time to think about the *bad* habits that hinder you. Think of a few *good* habits that could positively impact your dream life journey.

Consider how these three things—habits, routines, and environments—are either driving you closer or further away from your dreams, whether far away or simple ones.

One notable study from Duke University revealed that a staggering forty-five percent of our behavior is habitual and happens without us making conscious decision. Such findings beg the question: What if we could harness this force, directing forty-five percent of our day toward achieving our goals and dreams?

## Case Study: Peter Drucker

*"The best way to predict the future is to create it."*

*"There is nothing so useless as doing efficiently that which should not be done at all."*

*"Efficiency is doing things right; effectiveness is doing the right things."*

*"Knowledge has to be improved, challenged, and increased constantly, or it vanishes."*

*"Unless commitment is made, there are only promises and hopes... but no plans."*

*"We now accept the fact that learning is a lifelong process of keeping abreast of change. And the most pressing task is to teach people how to learn."*

*"Time is the scarcest resource and unless it is managed, nothing else can be managed."*

You've likely heard a few of these quotes before. All from Peter Drucker, the acclaimed management consultant and writer, who has unwavering belief in the power of habits and routines to achieve success.

Peter Drucker's mornings were a well-orchestrated blend of correspondence, reading, and writing, meticulously crafted to jumpstart his day. This routine wasn't just a series of tasks; it was a strategic approach to set the tone for productivity and effective time management. By prioritizing these activities each morning, Drucker ensured that his most critical tasks received the attention they deserved right at the start of his day.

In his personal life, Drucker mirrored this disciplined regimen. He wove exercise, reading, and quality time with family into his daily routine. This wasn't just about staying fit or leisure; it was a holistic approach to building an environment conducive to success. Drucker understood that a well-rounded routine, which balances professional work with personal well-being, forms the backbone of sustained productivity.

Imagine the impact of such a disciplined approach over time. Drucker's adherence to this structured routine set a high bar for personal achievement. Each day, he took deliberate steps toward his goals, culminating in a life marked by remarkable success. His story, unfolding through consistent habits, high standards, and a nurturing environment, stands as a compelling reminder of the power these elements hold in shaping both personal and professional triumphs.

***This isn't the sexy part of success, but the foundation upon which greatness is built.***

If we were to ask Peter Drucker what made him successful, the answer would most likely involve his consistent routines that prioritized his daily goals, excellent health habits, neat and clean environment, and the people and things he surrounded himself with.

The answer might leave some people wondering, *But what's the secret? Who did he know? Who gave him the money? His parents must have been successful.* But, often, it's the habits and environment that are the creators of that success. That is what it has been for me. If I wasn't willing to create a successful routine around one of my many dreams, then I needed to reassess how important that dream was to me in the first place.

## Understanding the Science Behind Habits

In the fall of 2020, after making the decision to leave college, I dove deep into the study of habits. This self-directed exploration became my alternative education, a journey through the works of renowned authors who have mastered the art of habit formation. Their insights replaced my conventional studies and provided a profound understanding of how habits shape our lives and our pursuit of dreams.

### High-Performance Habits

Brendon Burchard's "High-Performance Habits" brings to light the importance of clarity and energy. Visualize starting each day with a precise understanding of your goals, coupled with the energy to achieve them. This combination of clarity and vitality is crucial in forming habits that drive you toward success, laying the groundwork for a life filled with accomplishment.

## The Compound Effect

"The Compound Effect" by Darren Hardy introduces the transformative power of small, consistent actions. Every choice you make daily has the potential to incrementally build toward your dreams. It's the small steps, consistently taken, that create momentum, propelling you toward your aspirations.

## The Power of Habit

In "The Power of Habit" by Charles Duhigg, the science behind habit formation is unveiled. Understanding the cues and rewards that drive our actions allows us to reshape habits that hinder our goals. This knowledge enables you to turn your daily routine into a series of intentional actions leading to your dreams.

## The Seven Habits of Highly Effective People

Stephen Covey's "The Seven Habits of Highly Effective People" adds a vital layer to our habit-building journey. It's about developing habits that not only move you toward your goals but also reflect your personal ethics and character. These habits are the essence of who you are and who you become on the path to achieving your dreams.

## Atomic Habits

Lastly, "Atomic Habits" by James Clear, taught me that to truly change our habits, we must first change our identity. If I'm trying to "run daily" as a habit, I need to identify myself as a "runner". I need to buy running shoes, talk to runners, do things that runners do. Similarly, if someone is a smoker and they want to kick that habit - they must first shift their identity to say "I'm not a smoker". This makes it much easier to say no to others and to themselves when the urge arrises.

All of their insights into energy and productivity management are crucial. Keeping your energy high and focusing on your productivity is vital for sustaining momentum in achieving your dreams. This involves creating habits that enhance your physical and mental vitality, ensuring every day contributes positively to your journey.

Your environment, as underlined by each one of these authors, significantly influences habit formation. A conducive setting for positive habits is key. Whether it's a creatively stimulating workspace or a supportive social circle, your surroundings should reinforce the habits that will lead you to your dreams.

Through this self-directed study, I gained more than just an understanding of habits. I learned how to weave these principles into a cohesive strategy, transforming each day into a step toward a life where dreams are not distant hopes, but imminent realities.

Taking all of these learnings into consideration, I've created what I call the *backward walk*.

## The Backward Walk

This habit-focused way of thinking starts with our environment and traces it backward through our thoughts, actions, standards, and habits. By understanding this chain of events, we can gain a deeper understanding of our habits and, as a result, facilitate the meaningful change that we desire.

1. Habits                    4. Thoughts

2. Standards                 5. Environment

3. Actions

## 1. The Unconscious Nature of Habits

The journey to changing your life begins with understanding habits, which are actions performed regularly, often unconsciously. Here is a reminder of a critical insight: most of our daily decisions aren't actually decisions at all, but habits. These habitual actions, whether daily, weekly, or monthly, form the very fabric of our lives. While we might think our life is shaped by individual decisions, it's actually our habits that have a greater impact.

Here is a striking example: a sales team member who I worked with believed he had no habits, yet his morning routine revealed several unconscious habits that set him up for failure, or at least a harder path toward success. Small things, like hitting the snooze button, trying to figure out what to wear, and scrolling on his phone first thing in the morning all were daily and unconscious habits that added up to wasted time and energy that wasn't serving him any purpose in his pursuit of his Dream Life.

Before introducing new, positive habits, it's crucial to identify existing habits, especially those that may be holding us back. For instance, the routine of going to the bar every Friday night is a habit that shapes one's life. By identifying these patterns, we can begin to reshape them. The first step to changing your life, therefore, is to change your habits. I'd suggest logging your daily activities before bed to help recognize these patterns, including everything from waking up to what you eat, how you commute, and your evening activities. As fun as it may seem in the moment, the nose dive your productivity takes the day after might make that weekly trip to the bar less impressive. This detailed self-awareness is key to understanding the habits you already possess, paving the way for adding positive habits to transform your life.

## 2. Understanding Standards Versus Goals

The second understanding of the backward walk is the concept of standards and how they differ from goals. Standards are the benchmarks we set for ourselves. They represent the minimum level of performance or behavior that we accept from ourselves. A good example is adjusting workout routines. This transition from goal-setting (our aspiration) to establishing a workout routine (our standard) is crucial for building and sustaining habits that lead to life changes.

The practical approach to standards involves starting with manageable targets and gradually elevating them. For instance, if your aim is to develop a reading habit, you might begin by setting a standard to read one page per day. As this becomes ingrained, you can gradually increase the amount. By consistently meeting these standards, what once was an effort becomes a natural part of your daily routine, effectively turning a chosen action into a habit.

Standards are foundational for habit formation. By consciously choosing and adhering to our standards, even and especially when they're very small, we take control of our behaviors and, by extension, our lives. Setting an easily achievable standard at the beginning of your journey is the key to creating that habit. Identify your desired habits and integrate them as standards first.

## 3. Actions as the Foundation of Standards and Habits

The third part of the backward walk breaks down the significance of actions in shaping our lives. Our lives are a culmination of the actions we take daily. It is these actions that form the string of habits, which are underpinned by the standards we set. Understanding this chain of influence is crucial in recognizing the power of everyday actions in steering our lives toward accomplishing our dreams.

Identify and implement the actions necessary to meet your standards and form beneficial habits. For example, if the goal is to stop hitting the snooze button and wake up early, one must identify the actions that will make this possible, such as going to bed earlier or setting a specific and motivating reason to wake up. Things like preparing a gym bag the night before to ensure a morning workout, or placing a book in various locations to facilitate the habit of daily reading may be helpful. The idea is to 'booby-trap' oneself into completing these actions, thus making the achievement of standards and formation of habits almost inevitable.

Think deeply about the actions required to achieve your standards. This involves not just identifying the habit or standard but dissecting the underlying actions necessary for their realization. Again, if the standard is to exercise in the morning, one must plan actions like sleeping early and setting up exercise gear beforehand. It's a process of breaking down each goal into actionable steps and then embedding these steps into daily life.

## 4. Embracing the Power of Thoughts in Shaping Your Life

Understanding the impact of thoughts on our actions and, ultimately, on our lives is crucial in our journey to change our path. It's a fundamental truth that the thoughts we entertain on a daily basis shape our reality. As we've discussed the importance of habits and standards, it becomes evident that these are all influenced by our thoughts. Recognizing this connection is the first step in harnessing the power of thoughts to steer your life in the direction of your dreams.

Many of our thoughts are influenced by external factors—the media we consume, the conversations we have, the books we read (or don't read), and the people we surround ourselves with. These external stimuli have a profound impact on what occupies our minds and, consequently, the actions we take. For example, if you spend hours exposed to negative news, it's likely to affect your mindset and subsequent actions. It's essential to be mindful of these influences and strive to fill your mind with positive and constructive content.

Our upbringing and the environment we grow up in also shape our thought patterns. I, for instance, grew up in a small town where the prevailing belief was that rich people were inherently bad. This belief unconsciously influenced my actions and led to self-sabotage in my early business endeavors. It took years of therapy and emotional intelligence training to recognize and change this deep-seated belief (which turned out to not even be my own but the general belief of where I came from). This process underscores the importance of identifying and challenging negative thoughts that may be holding you back from achieving your full potential.

Your actions are a direct result of your thoughts. If you believe you can be successful, wealthy, or fit, your actions will naturally align with these beliefs. It's about cultivating a mindset that supports your aspirations. If you believe you are a failure, you will fail. I've "believed myself" out of college baseball, doing more musicals, and many other things in my life. So for you, this might involve journaling to identify your current thought patterns or intentionally seeking out conversations with people who embody the success you aspire to achieve.

To change your life, start by changing the narrative in your head. Surround yourself with people and content that uplift and inspire you. If your goal is financial success, engage with those who have achieved it. If it's fitness you're after, associate with those who prioritize health and well-being. These interactions will plant new seeds of thought, influencing your actions in a way that aligns with your goals.

Recognize that your daily thoughts dictate the actions you take and, in turn, shape your life. By consciously choosing positive and empowering thoughts, you set the stage for actions that drive you toward the life you desire. It's about creating a mental environment where your dreams can thrive, supported by thoughts that propel you forward.

## 5. Transforming Your Thoughts Through Environmental Influence

The fifth and final part of the backward walk addresses the profound impact your environment has on your thoughts, actions, and, ultimately, your life. This underscores another fundamental truth: your environment shapes your expectations and, as a result, your identity. Going back to the idea that we rise and fall to the expectations of our peer group, there's considerable truth to this. Your environment, from the people you surround yourself with to the places you frequent, sets the tone for your behavior and the standards you unconsciously adhere to.

Consider the example of military training. When placed in a group expected to run twenty miles, even those not in peak condition find themselves completing the task, driven by the collective expectation. Similarly, in a college setting where partying might be the norm, you might find yourself drawn into that lifestyle, not necessarily by choice but by environmental influence. The shift in environment, as seen in the COVID-19 pandemic, can have a transformative effect by changing these expectations and, consequently, your actions.

Your hometown or family environment also plays a critical role. For instance, growing up in a small town might instill the belief that wealth is negative or that constantly working on a passionate business startup is unhealthy. These ingrained beliefs can significantly impact your actions and decisions. When I moved to a larger city, I was initially influenced by my friends' habits, which, again, highlights the power of your immediate surroundings.

## Reverse Engineer Your Dreams

Recognizing the power of your environment is the first step in harnessing life to your advantage. Be mindful of where you are and who you're with, as these factors greatly influence your thoughts and actions. By deliberately choosing environments that align with your aspirations, you set yourself up for success and fulfillment beyond what you might have thought possible.

By applying the principles of the backward walk, starting with an awareness of our environments and then working backwards, we can unlock the full potential of our habits and harness their power in our quest for our own personal and professional success, and a life of fulfillment.

## Embracing the Power of Small Changes

Embracing the power of small changes is a pivotal theme in the journey of habit formation and self-improvement. The backwards walk through our habits, standards, actions, thoughts, and environment shows us how incremental adjustments in these areas can lead to significant transformations. As we acknowledge the challenges in modifying our habits and setting new standards, we understand the importance of small, consistent actions in creating a conducive environment for growth.

## Napoleon Bonaparte

Napoleon Bonaparte's story serves as a powerful example in this context. Rising from modest beginnings to become the Emperor of France, Napoleon was a military and strategic genius, renowned for his groundbreaking reforms and ambitious military campaigns. He significantly altered the political landscape of Europe, expanding the French Empire to its greatest territorial extent. Under his rule, Napoleon implemented widespread administrative and legal reforms, including the introduction of the Napoleonic Code, which has had a lasting influence on civil law systems around the world. He was a patron of the arts and sciences, fostering a cultural revolution that echoed the ideals of the Enlightenment.

His successes in battle, marked by innovative strategies and a deep understanding of warfare, earned him a reputation as one of history's greatest military leaders. Napoleon's achievements in building an empire, reforming a nation, and influencing European politics demonstrate the heights that can be reached with vision, ambition, and strategic acumen.

In his role as military leader, Napoleon developed the habit of very late nights, which then affected his ability to manage his empire effectively once he took over. This habit led to scattered leadership and, ultimately, to the demise of his empire and his life. This failure to adopt a more disciplined routine, to prioritize rest and recovery, illustrates how small habits can have outsized impacts on our lives. Just like Napoleon's late nights, our daily routines and habits, no matter how small, can significantly influence our ability to think clearly, make decisions, and achieve our dreams. By embracing small changes and aligning our actions with our aspirations, we can avoid the pitfalls of unproductive habits and set ourselves on a path to success.

## Reflection: A Powerful Tool for Growth

By carefully cultivating our environments, we can set the stage for developing habits that propel us toward our goals. As we navigate the journey of self-improvement and personal growth, it's essential to remember that the power of habit lies in the ability to shape our lives in profound ways. By understanding the chain of events that leads to habit formation, we can take control of our destinies and chart a course toward a future filled with success, fulfillment, and happiness.

The backward walk concept provides an invaluable tool for understanding and transforming our habits, empowering us to make meaningful changes that propel us toward our aspirations.

By nurturing these concepts, we can unlock our full potential and create the life we've always envisioned. However, in our pursuit of success, we must recognize the importance of celebrating our accomplishments and reflecting on our progress.

Building on the insights from our exploration of habits, routines, and environments, we now turn to the transformative power of reflection. This next chapter explores how reflecting on our progress, both significant and subtle, can amplify our motivation and sharpen our strategies. Through introspection, we gain the ability to recalibrate our approach, ensuring that our actions are in harmony with our evolving goals. This practice is essential in enhancing our journey toward success, drawing from the lessons we've learned and the growth we've achieved.

# CHAPTER 13

## Celebrating and Reflecting on Your Awesome S#!t

In the annals of human achievement, few stories resonate quite like Sir Edmund Hillary's triumphant ascent of Mount Everest as discussed in Chapter 7. This historic feat serves as a powerful testament to the importance of celebrating our accomplishments to build momentum for future successes. As we work toward living the life of our dreams, it's crucial to recognize the role that celebration and reflection play in our growth and development. Sir Edmund Hillary's awe-inspiring expedition to the summit of the world's tallest peak provides a poignant example of this principle.

Hillary and Tenzing Norgay, his Nepalese Sherpa guide, reached the summit of Mount Everest on May 29, 1953. Their incredible achievement culminated from years of training, planning, and perseverance. Yet, the story doesn't end there. Upon descending back down the mountain, Hillary and Norgay were greeted with jubilant celebration and lauded for their courage and determination. This recognition validated their efforts and gave them new energy for their next adventure. Hillary then parlayed this fame into many interviews, books, and world fame.

Just as Hillary and Norgay reveled in their hard-earned success, we must also learn to embrace the moments of triumph in our lives, even when not as grand as climbing Mount Everest. Doing so creates a positive feedback loop that encourages us to continue striving to greater heights. Celebrating our achievements is more than just basking in the glory of our victories. It's an opportunity to:

◆ Reflect on the journey that brought you to this point.

◆ Assess the challenges you've overcome.

◆ Appreciate the lessons learned along the way and apply to other areas of life.

It's crucial for you to actively engage in celebrating your achievements to create a self-reinforcing cycle of success and motivation. This involves more than just acknowledging your victories; it requires a deliberate process of reflection and assessment. Start by taking time to ponder the journey that led to your achievements. Think about the initial challenges, the hurdles you faced, and how you overcame them. This reflection helps you recognize your resilience and adaptability. Next, appreciate the lessons each step of the journey taught you.

These lessons are invaluable as they prepare you for future challenges and contribute to your personal growth. By doing this, you not only honor your achievements but also set the stage for continued success and self-improvement. This process of reflection, assessment, and appreciation turns each victory, big or small, into a stepping stone for future achievements, fostering a mindset geared toward ongoing growth and accomplishment.

## The Power of Positive Reinforcement

Positive reinforcement is an often overlooked yet undeniably potent force in the grand tapestry of personal and professional success. Serving as a catalyst for building momentum and maintaining motivation, acknowledging your achievements can transform your journey toward realizing your dreams.

As we explore the myriad stories of those who have reached dizzying heights of accomplishment, a common thread emerges: the power of positive reinforcement. By celebrating our victories, big and small, we cultivate an environment in which motivation flourishes and momentum builds. This continuous cycle of recognition and affirmation allows us to push the boundaries of what we believe is possible.

As sweet as the whole world celebrating something you've done can be, imagine for a moment a world in which Sir Edmund Hillary had climbed Mount Everest but received no accolades for his extraordinary feat.

In that world, he'd need to understand the essential role of self-celebration in personal achievement. While external accolades undoubtedly add to the sweetness of success, the true power lies within our own recognition and celebration of our triumphs. You, as an achiever in your own right, can harness this power by actively acknowledging and rejoicing in your accomplishments, regardless of external validation.

Self-celebration begins with internal acknowledgment. After achieving a goal, take a moment to pause and genuinely congratulate yourself. Reflect on the effort, dedication, and perseverance it took to reach this point. Allow yourself to feel proud of what you've accomplished. This can be as simple as writing down your achievement in a journal, treating yourself to something special, or just taking a moment of quiet to savor the success.

Furthermore, sharing your victories with close friends, family, or even a personal diary can amplify this sense of achievement. These acts of self-celebration create a positive feedback loop in your mind, reinforcing your belief in your abilities and encouraging you to set and pursue even higher goals.

In essence, whether the world recognizes your achievements or not, taking the time to celebrate your own successes is crucial for sustained motivation and future triumphs. Just as Hillary's celebrated ascent of Everest propelled him to further achievements, your own self-recognition and celebration can be the springboard for your continued success and personal growth.

# The Power of Momentum in Motivation

Positive reinforcement is a powerful tool for building momentum and maintaining motivation. By consciously acknowledging and celebrating our achievements, we can propel ourselves forward, fueled by the energy and confidence that comes from recognizing our greatness.

One of my favorite quotes come from Alex Hormozi, in which he says:

> *"Confidence doesn't come from telling yourself you can do something, it comes from an undeniable stack of evidence that you are who you say you are."*

You must be willing to admire and appreciate the things you *have* accomplished up to this point in order to truly have the self-confidence to pursue "bigger" things or anything outside of your comfort zone.

## The Check Six Program:
### Boosting Morale and Performance

The annals of history brim with tales of accomplishments, often centered on the individuals. Yet, there exist plenty of examples of organizations that harness the power of recognizing, celebrating, and reflecting on achievements to achieve even greater success. Two examples are the U.S. Navy's Check Six program during World War II and the Kaizen philosophy implemented at Toyota in the 1980s.

The Check Six program, masterminded by Admiral Chester Nimitz, was conceived as a morale booster and performance enhancer for Navy pilots during World War II. The program celebrated pilots who successfully shot down enemy planes by painting the pilot's name on the side of the aircraft, constantly reminding them of their accomplishments. This tangible recognition of their feat instilled a deep pride, fueling the desire to achieve even more. The Check Six program proved so effective that it played a crucial role in the U.S. Navy's ultimate victory in the Pacific.

## The Kaizen Philosophy:
### Driving Continuous Improvement at Toyota

Half a world away and a few decades later, the Kaizen philosophy took root at Toyota, reshaping the automobile manufacturer's approach to efficiency and productivity. Kaizen, which emphasizes continuous improvement, was implemented to recognize and celebrate incremental progress, driving the company toward more tremendous success. Employees were encouraged to identify and address small inefficiencies in their work processes, and upon succeeding, would be recognized and celebrated before their peers. This culture of celebration served as a constant reminder of their achievements, motivating them to continue striving for excellence. The Kaizen philosophy was instrumental in significantly improving Toyota's manufacturing operations and played a vital role in the company becoming one of the world's largest and most successful automobile manufacturers.

## The Profound Importance of Recognizing and Reflecting on Accomplishments

To apply the powerful lessons of recognition and celebration from the Check Six program and Kaizen philosophy in your personal journey, consider these actionable steps:

1. **Personal Achievement Recognition**: Similar to the Check Six program, where pilots' achievements were visibly acknowledged, create a personal system to recognize your successes. This could be as simple as maintaining a journal where you jot down your accomplishments, no matter how small. Alternatively, you could have a physical 'achievement board' in your home or office where you note or display symbols of your achievements.

2. **Celebrate Incremental Progress**: Embrace the Kaizen philosophy of valuing continuous improvement by acknowledging and celebrating your small victories and dreams. Recognize the steps you take toward a larger goal. For instance, if your goal is to write a book, truly go celebrate each chapter completed. These small celebrations keep you motivated and remind you of the progress you're making.

3. **Tangible Reminders:** Just as pilots had their names painted on aircraft, create tangible reminders of your achievements. It could be a certificate you make for yourself, a small trophy, or even a celebratory ritual.

These physical manifestations of success serve as constant motivation.

4. **Share Your Success**: Share your achievements with friends, family, or colleagues. Just as Toyota employees were recognized before their peers, sharing your success with your support network can enhance your sense of accomplishment and provide additional motivation. As much as our society despises the "likes culture" of social media, those likes and comments are constant reminders that you are who you say you are. Or better yet, you are becoming that person one step at a time.

5. **Reflect and Adapt:** Regularly reflect on your accomplishments, pondering what they mean to you and how they contribute to your larger goals. This reflection can be done through journaling, meditation, or discussions with mentors or peers. Use these reflections to adapt and refine your future goals and strategies.

By actively incorporating these elements of recognition, celebration, and reflection into your life, you can create a positive feedback loop that boosts morale, increases motivation, and propels you toward achieving even greater successes.

## Personal Development and Productivity Literature

In our journey toward realizing our dreams, the power of recognizing, celebrating, and reflecting on our accomplishments cannot be overstated. This concept, championed by influential authors such as Charles Dugigg in "The Power of Habit", Brendon

Burchard in "High-Performance Habits", and Darren Hardy in "The Compound Effect" demonstrates how acknowledging both big and small wins can create a momentum that propels us toward greater achievements. Hardy's narrative reveals how each small success, when compounded over time, can lead to significant transformations in our lives. It's about using each victory, no matter its size, to build an upward trajectory toward our goals.

Stephen Covey, in "The Seven Habits of Highly Effective People," echoes the importance of this practice. He contends that taking the time to recognize and reflect on our achievements is crucial for maintaining a balanced life. This balance allows us to pursue personal and professional goals in harmony, ensuring that our successes in one area don't come at the cost of another. It's about creating a life where every aspect works in unison toward our overarching aspirations.

The perspective of Brené Brown in "The Gifts of Imperfection" adds another layer to this idea. Brown emphasizes the significance of acknowledging progress as a means to bolster self-worth and build resilience. Recognizing our progress, as Dane Espegard, the dreams guy, says, "is happiness." This simple act of acknowledging our growth fosters a sense of fulfillment and joy in our daily endeavors.

Robin Sharma, in "The 5 AM Club," and James Clear, in "Atomic Habits," offer practical advice on how to incorporate celebration into our routines. Sharma advocates for daily reflection and celebration as part of our morning rituals, setting a positive tone for the day. Clear, on the other hand, focuses on the importance of rewarding ourselves for our successes, establishing a positive feedback loop that encourages continuous progress.

Lastly, David Allen, through "Getting Things Done: The Art of Stress-Free Productivity," reminds us that celebrating accomplishments is essential for maintaining high motivation levels. By acknowledging our achievements, we fuel our drive to tackle tasks effectively, thereby maintaining a balanced and productive life.

By absorbing the wisdom of these authors and applying it to our lives, we build a solid foundation for success. This foundation is not just built on achieving goals but also on recognizing the journey toward those goals, celebrating every milestone, and reflecting on the lessons learned. This approach ensures a life of continuous growth, satisfaction, and achievement, where every success, big or small, is a step toward realizing our ultimate dreams.

## Really, Celebrate and Reflect on Your Awesome S#!t

A study conducted by the "Harvard Business Review" discovered that acknowledging and celebrating small wins daily can significantly enhance employee motivation, morale, and productivity. Recognizing someone's effort, achievement, and productivity will boost it up to one hundred percent. These findings resemble the importance of incorporating celebration into workplace culture just like Toyota has, ensuring that employees feel seen and appreciated for their efforts, and how that can parlay into other areas of their lives.

Create a ritual around celebrating your achievements. This could be as simple as marking off completed goals on your Dreams List, or perhaps sharing your successes with a supportive friend or family member. The act of sharing not only reinforces your accomplishment but also builds a supportive network that appreciates your journey.

Reflect on the journey behind each achievement. Consider what it took to get there – the challenges you overcame, the skills you developed, and the resilience you demonstrated. This reflection not only enhances your sense of achievement but also provides valuable insights for future endeavors.

Additionally, integrate the practices suggested by Brené Brown, Robin Sharma, and James Clear. Embrace Brown's advice on recognizing progress to maintain self-worth, incorporate Sharma's idea of daily reflection into your routine, and follow Clear's suggestion to create a positive feedback loop by rewarding yourself for successes.

Finally, as the Harvard Business Review study suggests, these practices of acknowledgment and celebration aren't just feel-good actions; they're backed by empirical evidence showing their impact on motivation and productivity. By actively recognizing and celebrating each step you take on your Dreams List, you create an environment of continuous growth and self-motivation, turning the journey toward your dreams into a fulfilling and rewarding process.

## Stay Grounded and Present in Your Journey

As we transition into the final chapter of this book, we will look at the profound, yet often misunderstood concept of legacy. Legacy, the notion of leaving a lasting impact on the world, is both inspiring and intimidating. It's a concept that can evoke feelings of pressure and anxiety as we grapple with the desire to make a mark that endures beyond our lifetime. However, by embracing the practices of recognizing, celebrating, and reflecting on our accomplishments, we can alleviate this pressure and find momentum in our journey toward creating a meaningful legacy.

But let's pause and ponder some challenging questions before we move on.

### *What if the legacy is an illusion?*

### *What if the impact we strive to leave behind is inevitably forgotten over time?*

### *Would this realization change the way we approach our daily lives?*

In the final chapter, we will explore these intriguing questions about legacy. We will examine what it truly means to leave a lasting impression, how it influences our pursuit of dreams, both big and small, and, ultimately, what legacy could mean to you in a life dedicated to achieving your deepest aspirations.

We will untangle the complexities of legacy, redefining it in the context of a life well-lived and dreams passionately pursued *today*.

# CHAPTER 14
## Legacy Isn't Real?

Andrew Carnegie was born in Scotland in 1835 and immigrated to the United States as a child. From working as a bobbin boy in a cotton factory to becoming a telegrapher and eventually a leading industrialist, Carnegie epitomized the American dream. By the late 19th century, he had built Carnegie Steel into the largest steel company in the world.

Despite his immense success, Carnegie might best be remembered for his commitment to philanthropy, articulated in his 1889 essay "The Gospel of Wealth." In this influential piece, Carnegie argued that the affluent have a moral obligation to distribute their wealth in ways that promote the welfare and happiness of the common man. This philosophy guided the latter part of his life.

Carnegie began systematically reducing his own wealth by funding the establishment of libraries, schools, universities, and various public institutions across the United States, Britain, and other parts of the world. By the time of his death in 1919, Carnegie had given away about $350 million, which is equivalent to billions in today's dollars.

Reflecting on his life, Carnegie believed that his greatest achievement was not the steel empire he created but the opportunities he provided through his philanthropic endeavors. His legacy is not just in the physical libraries and institutions that bear his name but in his role in promoting the concept of philanthropy and public giving.

Andrew Carnegie's story, demonstrates a profound shift from wealth accumulation to wealth distribution, underscoring a realization in his later years that true legacy is built through the betterment of society, not just the amassing of personal fortunes.

This narrative of transformation and giving sets the stage for an unconventional yet profound exploration of the concept of legacy. In this chapter, we will challenge the traditional notion that legacy is the ultimate goal in life and instead propose that a purposeful life aligned with our values and dreams is far more fulfilling than the relentless pursuit of success, wealth, and family legacy that many are currently chasing, whether they realize that's what they're after or not.

## The True Measure of a Life Well Lived

The following stories serve as a reminder that success and wealth are not the only path to a meaningful life. The accurate measure of a life well-lived lies not in the monuments we build or the accolades we accumulate but in the values we embody and the connections we forge along the way. It's the little dreams as much as the big ones.

So, as we venture into this thought-provoking exploration of legacy and its place in our lives, let us ponder the possibility that our most significant contributions may not be etched in stone or immortalized in history books but instead woven into the fabric of our relationships, our experiences, and the lives we touch along the way. And perhaps, in the end, that is the most authentic and lasting legacy any of us can hope to achieve.

## Your Pursuits On The Stand

Jim Thorpe's life and achievements exemplify a legacy built on versatility, resilience, and sheer talent. Known as one of the most versatile athletes in modern sports history, Thorpe's accomplishments spanned across various disciplines, each marked by extraordinary success.

In the 1912 Olympic Games in Stockholm, Thorpe won two gold medals, one in the Decathlon and another in the Pentathlon. His performance in these events was nothing short of remarkable, showcasing his exceptional athleticism and endurance. These Olympic victories placed him among the elite athletes of his time and etched his name in the annals of Olympic history.

Beyond the Olympic arena, Thorpe's athletic prowess extended to professional baseball and football. He played Major League Baseball for several teams, including the New York Giants, the Cincinnati Reds, and the Boston Braves, demonstrating his remarkable adaptability and skill in different sports realms.

In professional football, Thorpe's impact was equally significant. He played for several teams and was a founding member of the American Professional Football Association (APFA), which later became the National Football League (NFL). His presidency of the APFA marked a significant contribution to the development and organization of professional football in the United States.

He was among the most successful athletes of all time, in multiple sports and the Olympics, and is arguably the founding father of the National Football League. Yet today, very few know who Jim Thorpe is. It takes the right person in the right trivia environment to know his name.

Jim Thorpe's story poignantly illustrates that even the most remarkable achievements can fade into obscurity over time. Despite his extraordinary success in multiple sports and his pivotal role in the founding of the NFL, his legacy has dimmed, reminding us that fame and recognition are often transient, even for the greatest achievers.

## Echoes of Forgotten Legends:
## The Transience of Fame

Take Harry Vardon. He was a golf legend from the early 20th century. Harry won the British Open a record six times between 1896 and 1914.

He was known for his innovative grip and elegant swing. Vardon's influence on the sport was immense. However, as the years passed, his name gradually receded from the public consciousness, overshadowed by more recent golfing greats like Arnold Palmer and Tiger Woods.

The only people who know Harry Vardon are golf super fans or trivia masters.

Paavo Nurmi was a dominant force in long-distance running during the 1920s. The Finnish athlete won nine remarkable Olympic gold medals and set numerous world records. Despite his extraordinary accomplishments, Nurmi's fame gradually waned, and today, his name is only barely recognized, even in the niche world of long-distance running.

William Randolph Hearst was a powerful newspaper magnate and media tycoon. His influence on journalism and politics was immense and cannot be understated during the early 20th century. His sensationalist approach to news reporting earned him both fortune and authority. However, as the decades passed, Hearst's empire dwindled, and his once-illustrious name faded from public consciousness.

Peggy Guggenheim, an art collector and patron, significantly promoted modern art during the mid-20th century. She amassed an extraordinary collection of works by prominent artists such as Picasso, Kandinsky, and Pollock. Despite her influence on art, her name is not widely remembered today.

Al Capp, the creator of the world famous comic strip *Li'l Abner*, reached the pinnacle of fame during the 1940s and 1950s. His satirical and witty take on American culture made him a household name. But as tastes shifted and new comic artists emerged, Capp's star faded from fame and memory.

Croesus, an ancient king of Lydia, was renowned for his immense wealth and extravagance. His name has become synonymous with riches, but his story has largely been lost to history, known mainly to scholars of antiquity.

Polycrates, a powerful and prosperous ruler of the Greek island of Samos during the sixth century BCE, was known for his luxurious lifestyle and ambitious building projects. His reign ended abruptly when he was betrayed and killed, leaving his once-great empire to crumble into obscurity.

## A Reflection on Success and Its Impermanence

These compelling stories remind us that success—whether financial or other—and fame are very often fleeting. Focusing on living a purposeful life aligned with our own personal values is far more critical than pursuing wealth and authority for the sake of believing that we will leave a lasting legacy somewhere, even within our own families.

## Challenging Conventional Wisdom

True success isn't about financial gains or widespread fame. It's about living a life that's true to your values, a life that's more fulfilling than any pursuit of wealth or authority. You don't need financial freedom to do what you want; you already possess exactly what you need to live the life of your dreams. You see, it's autonomy that truly matters – the freedom to live your life on your terms, regardless of your financial status.

## Chasing Money Is Keeping Your Spirit Poor

Freedom is often misconstrued as financial independence, but true freedom is already yours. It's about living life according to your values and desires. This realization dawned on me when I noticed how people, including myself, often fall into the trap of pursuing financial freedom, believing it's the key to a fulfilling life. But, in truth, it's **autonomy** that grants us the ability to do what we love, with whom we want, whenever we want.

This revelation reshaped my understanding of success. I've seen people choose careers like medicine or law, believing these paths would lead to wealth. But, often, this comes at the cost of their personal freedom and happiness. If you're doing something solely for the money, you're not really free. You're missing out on the joy of autonomy–doing what you love every day. It's not worth being financially free if you hate what you're doing. We all have a finite time on this Earth, and it's essential to spend every day doing what we genuinely love.

I encourage you to rethink your relationship with money and success. Start by assessing your basic needs and expenses. I once read about a musician who gave up a lucrative corporate job to pursue his passion. He lived frugally, working as a taxi driver to cover his expenses, and dedicating most of his time to his music. He also loved the time he spent driving cab, connecting with new people and hearing their stories. His time was split between two passions, and no matter the financial outcomes, he loved every second of every day of his life. This story is a powerful example of prioritizing passion over profit. It gives me chills! It's about breaking free from the time-for-money trap that society conditions us into and finding joy in pursuing what truly matters to you.

Finally, I urge you to think deeply about what success means to you. It's not about the monetary value attached to your time; it's about pursuing what you're passionate about, regardless of the financial returns. Success is waking up every day excited about what you're going to do, not feeling burdened by the expectation of financial gains. As you reflect on your path to success, remember that the true measure of a life well-lived is not in wealth or fame, but in the joy and fulfillment found in living true to your passions and values.

What will your wildest dreams be, if they don't center around amassing wealth? What would you do with your life? Your *legacy?*

## Examining Lives and Legacies

By examining the lives of the remarkable yet largely forgotten figures from previous chapters, we can glean insights into the true nature of legacy and its place in our lives. It becomes clear that it isn't the accolades or wealth we accumulate that define our lasting impact, but rather the meaningful connections we forge and the values we uphold. For you, as a reader seeking to create your own legacy, this insight is crucial.

To leave a legacy that endures, focus on living a life that resonates deeply with your core values. Ask yourself, what are the principles and beliefs that you hold dear? How can your daily actions reflect these values? The legacy you leave should be a reflection of the life you live, imbued with purpose and intentionality.

Consider the relationships you nurture and the lives you touch. The most enduring legacies are often those that positively impact others. Whether it's through acts of kindness, mentorship, or giving back to your community, these interactions create ripples that extend far beyond your immediate circle.

Reflect on how you can use your talents, passions, and resources to make a meaningful difference. It could be through your professional work, volunteer efforts, or simply by being a supportive friend or family member. Every action you take that aligns with your values contributes to the legacy you are building.

Lastly, embrace the idea that your legacy is not just about the end of your life, but about how you live each day. It's in the choices you make, the people you help, and the way you conduct yourself in the face of challenges. By living authentically and with purpose, you naturally create a legacy that is not only fulfilling but also enduring. This is the legacy that truly matters, one that transcends material achievements and resides in the hearts and memories of those whose lives you've touched.

## Embracing the Infinite Game of Life

In our journey to live a full life, it's crucial to understand it as an 'Infinite Game,' a concept eloquently described by Simon Sinek. This perspective sees life not as a series of finite goals or achievements but as a continuous journey of growth, contribution, and the pursuit of a higher purpose. As you navigate this path, consider how you can play this infinite game in a way that aligns with your deepest values and leaves a positive imprint on the world.

Consider how you can infuse your daily life with actions and choices that reflect your core values and beliefs. This isn't about grand gestures, but consistent, small acts that collectively build a narrative of who you are and what you stand for. Your legacy is built day by day, through every choice you make and every interaction you have.

Furthermore, embrace the concept of lifelong learning and growth. The infinite game mindset encourages continuous personal development, not just for your benefit but for the enrichment of those around you. As you learn and grow, you become better equipped to contribute positively to the lives of others, thereby enhancing your legacy.

Remember, playing the infinite game of life isn't about reaching any final destination or accumulating a list of achievements. It's about *how* you play the game—with integrity, purpose, and a focus on the bigger picture. By doing so, you ensure that your legacy is not just a memory of what you achieved, but a living testament to the values and principles that guided your life.

## Ancient Wisdom for Modern Lifestyle Design

I also want to dive into the age-old wisdom of the Book of Ecclesiastes, a text that transcends religious boundaries with its universal themes of wisdom, wealth, pleasure, work, and the passage of time. This ancient text, dating back thousands of years, still holds profound relevance to our modern lives, offering insights into the human experience that resonate across ages and cultures.

Ecclesiastes, traditionally attributed to King Solomon, presents a core message that is strikingly contemporary: the pursuit of material wealth, pleasure, and professional success alone often leads to a sense of futility. This resonates with this chapter about legacy and purposeful living, highlighting that a life solely focused on transient achievements might miss out on deeper fulfillment.

What Ecclesiastes emphasizes, and what aligns with our exploration of legacy, is the importance of living a life grounded in purpose and value. This doesn't necessarily mean adhering to religious commandments; instead, it's about understanding that chasing external success without internal fulfillment often leads to a sense of emptiness. Whether one is spiritual, religious, or neither, this message underscores the significance of aligning our actions with our core values and the impact we wish to have on the world.

By considering the teachings of Ecclesiastes, we are encouraged to reflect on our own lives. Are we pursuing things that bring true satisfaction and align with our deeper values, or are we caught up in the vanity of ephemeral successes? I invite you to contemplate the essence of a meaningful life—one that balances the pursuit of personal ambitions with a commitment to living authentically and making a lasting, positive impact on those around us.

In essence, the wisdom of Ecclesiastes serves as a timeless guide, urging us to examine our lives and choices through the lens of purpose and value. It's a call to live intentionally, focusing on what truly matters and cultivating a legacy that extends beyond material accomplishments to the very quality of our lives and the lives we touch.

## Integrating Ancient Wisdom with Modern Dreams

In this context, the Dreams List becomes an essential tool, not just for setting goals but for aligning our daily actions with a purpose that transcends mere material success. It encourages us to reflect deeply on what truly matters to us, beyond the temporary allure of wealth and accolades. This blueprint for success in lifestyle design is about more than achieving specific goals; it's about creating a life imbued with meaning, satisfaction, and a sense of contribution.

We can use the Dreams List as a guide to prioritize experiences, relationships, and personal growth that align with our core values. This approach ensures that our pursuit of dreams goes hand in hand with a life of purpose and significance, as suggested by the timeless wisdom of Ecclesiastes.

Thus, as we've gone deeper into the concept of the Dreams List, I hope it is clear that the impact of living a life true to our values and purpose is the key. Our Dreams List becomes not just a checklist of objectives but a map guiding us toward a life that is rich in experiences, relationships, and personal fulfillment—a true embodiment of a well-designed one life.

## Three Core Components for a Purpose-Driven Life

1. Setting clear goals based on deeply held values.

2. Nurturing a positive mindset that allows for the pursuit of those goals.

3. Aligning one's daily routine with the dreams and goals one is pursuing.

When these elements are thoughtfully combined, they provide a robust foundation and formula upon which a life that is not only successful but also profoundly fulfilling and purpose-driven can be created.

## Building Your Dream Life

It is not enough to simply appreciate or understand the Dreams concepts. True transformation and growth occur when we actively integrate these principles into our daily lives. As we embrace this journey of self-discovery and purposeful living, it's important to remember that we must continually commit to the process of refining our goals, mindset, and routines to better align with our values. This goes back to *Chapter 1*. As human beings today, we have so many opportunities and tools to allow us to pursue the fantastic life of our dreams.

## A Life of Purpose, Joy, and Meaningful Dreams

As we conclude this journey, I hope it's clear that living a life of purpose and fulfillment isn't just an aspiration but an achievable reality. Each chapter of this book has been a stepping stone toward understanding and realizing your dreams, aligning with your deepest values, and living each day with intention and fulfillment.

From Chapters 2 and 3, you've learned the art of allocating time and money, understanding these as crucial currencies, and we pre-handled any objection you could have to the Dreams List lifestyle. The Strangest Secret and The Ambition Habit chapters have equipped you with the knowledge that your life is a reflection of your thoughts and ambitions, created by your habits. With the creation of your Dreams List, you have a clear roadmap to navigate through life's different stages, categorizing and chasing dreams that resonate with your heart and soul.

The subsequent chapters have taken you deeper into making these dreams a reality. Through effective time management, harnessing energy, and building empowering habits, you're now equipped to turn your aspirations into tangible achievements. The importance of celebrating these milestones, as discussed in Chapter 13, is pivotal in maintaining motivation and recognizing the progress you've made.

As we explored in this final chapter, 'Legacy Isn't Real,' the pursuit of dreams is not about leaving a mark for posterity but about creating a life that is rich in experiences, relationships, and personal growth. Your legacy is defined by the joy you find and spread, the lives you touch, and the fulfillment you derive from every moment.

## Your Call to Action: Live Your Dream Life Now

Now, as you close this book, the real work begins. Your call to action is clear: Start living your Dream Life today. Revisit your Dreams List regularly, refine it, and let it be your compass. Celebrate your progress, however small, and remember that each step forward is a victory. Be mindful of your time, manage your energy wisely, and cultivate habits that propel you toward your goals. Embrace the journey with all its highs and lows, for it is in this journey that the essence of a truly extraordinary life lies.

Remember, the most meaningful legacy you can leave is a life lived with passion, purpose, empathy, and joy. As you move forward, carry with you the lessons from this book and let them guide you in designing a life that is not only successful by your own standards but also deeply fulfilling and joyful.

So, go ahead, make your mark on the world in your unique way, and go do awesome s#!t, all the time. Your Dream Life awaits!

### Thank you for reading!

My name is Alex Funk, and I believe in a world where everyone has a Dreams List.

Here's how you can help bring that world to life:

1. Start dreaming! Use this book as your launchpad into your Dream Life. For all resources and to connect with me/follow for more Dream Life tools go to: alexrfunk.com

2. If you're willing… leaving this book a 5-star Amazon review will help tremendously in getting the message in more hands and hearts!

> *Anyone who leaves a review, send a screenshot to alex@thedreamslist.com and we will set up a FREE Dream Life planning session with you to help you implement!*

3. Pass this book/message along! Dream out loud!

Turn the page for 400+ examples to add to your first Dreams List (after you leave a review? 😊 ).

# DREAMS I'VE CROSSED OFF (FIRST FIVE YEARS)

*First Dreams Retreat: August 12, 2019*
Got it **started**. (15 dreams)

1. Learned how to start a passive income - Oct. 2019

2. Helped my brother get his Rooftop brand going - Oct. 2019

3. Helped my mom finish her kitchen remodel - Dec. 2019

4. Got a new car without taking out a loan - Dec. 2019

5. Beat my friend Jack Ryan in chess - January 2020

6. Went to Mexico (Cabo San Lucas) - January 2020

7. Went deep sea fishing - January 2020

8. Learned how to buy a house - Spring 2020

9. Learned to meditate - March 2020

10. Got a life coach - April 2020

11. Earned the Vector Marketing national trip - June 2020

12. Spoke at our SC2 conference - July 2020

13. Ran a branch office with Vector - Summer 2020

14. Ran a top 10 branch office at that - Summer 2020

15. Never let money be the motivator in my work - Summer 2020

*Second Dreams Retreat: August 12, 2020*
*Implemented the Google* **doc** *for the first time*
*(55 dreams)*

1. Bought Lululemon clothes - Aug. 2020

2. Bought Apple stock - Aug. 2020

3. Went skydiving - Aug. 2020

4. Visited my brother in Arizona and relaxed there - Aug. 2020

5. Rode ATVs in the AZ desert - August 2020

6. Saw both stadiums there - August 2020

7. Upgraded my posture (for Zoom working) - Aug. 2020

8. Donated $100 in the year - Sept. 2020

9. Visited my cousin Ben in Atlanta - Sept. 2020

10. Continued the life coaching with Mike Chu into the EVOLVE program - Sept. 2020

11. Learned to Bible study from my mom - Sept. 2020

12. Made meditating a daily habit for a month - Oct. 2020

13. Learned how to cook on my own (well) from my dad - Nov. 2020

14. Bought a house - Nov. 2020

15. Visited my sister in Colorado - Nov. 2020

16. Saw both stadiums in Denver - November 2020

17. Was featured on Vector's Instagram - Nov. 2020

18. Went on a hunting trip with my dad and uncles in Montana - Nov. 2020

19. Got a treadmill - Nov. 2020

20. Kicked the habit of biting my fingernails - Dec. 2020

21. Was the best gift giver at Funk Christmas - Dec. 2020

22. Ran a marathon - Dec. 2020

23. Talked to Bruce Goodman - Dec. 2020

24. Read 10 books - Dec. 2020

25. Never did any drugs - All year 2020

26. Did not succumb to my housemates drinking 2x per weekend - All year 2020

27. Never felt like I was working a day in my life - All year 2020

28. Never did any drugs - All year 2021

29. Developed a daily prayer habit - All year 2021

30. Talked to my sister on the phone at least weekly about anything random (which got our relationship back and in a great place) - All year 2021

31. Never felt like I was working a day in my life - All year 2021

32. Successfully leased out my house to house hack - January 2021

33. Visited my friends in Duluth - January 2021

34. Did create a dream wife exercise (via Danny Lewis) - January 2021

35. Visited Jack Ryan in Colorado - February 2021

36. Saw the Rocky mountains - February 2021

37. Climbed a mountain - February 2021

38. Went skiing in Colorado - February 2021

39. Went to the Coors factory - February 2021

40. Saw where a famous movie was filmed - February 2021

41. Went to Gulf Shores, AL - March 2021

42. Learned how to edit photos like my friend Colleen Dolan - March 2021

43. Started going to church again - March 2021

44. Went to Hawaii - March 2021

45. Swam with sharks in Hawaii - March 2021

46. Had a pina colada in Hawaii - March 2021

47. Touched a palm tree in Hawaii - March 2021

48. Saw Pearl Harbor - March 2021

49. Swam in the Pacific Ocean - March 2021

50. Took singing lessons - April 2021

51. Bought dress shirts from Grant Paterakos - April 2021

52. Found my faith again at a high level - May 2021

53. Felt good in my own skin - May 2021

54. Bought a computer monitor - July 2021

55. Reached 80 WPM typing - July 2021

***Third*** *Dreams Retreat: August 7, 2021*
*Implemented the Google* ***spreadsheet*** *for the first time (25 dreams)*

1. Felt comfortable with being successful - August 2021

2. Had a legal drink at Manny's Steakhouse - August 2021

3. Figured out my financial freedom numbers - August 2021

4. Had a road map to financial freedom planned - August 2021

5. Was in a wedding - August 2021

6. Bought my 2nd house - August 2021

7. Bought a property to Airbnb - August 2021

8. Purchased a property with my parents - August 2021

9. Got a record player - August 2021

10. Sold Cutco from behind the booth - August 2021

11. Learned how Dane is such a great dad FIRST and THEN business leader second - Summer 2021

12. Went to South Dakota - September 2021

13. Cracked an egg with one hand - September 2021

14. Drank a gallon of water for one year straight - September 2021

15. Did my morning routine one month straight - September 2021

16. Ran my first Airbnb - September 2021

17. Crossed off more dreams every year than the year before - September 2021

18. Never missed an EVOLVE retreat - September 2021

19. Went on a trip with Elliot James - September 2021

20. Visited Colleen in Austin, TX - September 2021

21. Met Lydia Frentsos in person - September 2021

22. Met Ana Tsiskarishvili in person - September 2021

23. Found my dream girl - September 2021

24. Was featured on the CLSK podcast episode - September 2021

25. Did Bible study with Jon Paulson - October 2021

***Fourth** Dreams Retreat: October 12, 2021 (virtually)*
*Added the Dreams **Planning** tab to my sheet (99 dreams)*

1. Reached 1000 dreams on my Dreams List - October 2021

2. Gave Adam an American experience before he leaves (my Asian roommate, took to MN Vikings game) - October 2021

3. Unfollowed all the people I didn't care about on Instagram - October 2021

4. Owned a week's worth of oversized hoodies like the one Elliot had on at the dreams retreat - October 2021

5. Upgraded my calls with Mike Chu so I got three calls/ month - October 2021

6. Talked to a counselor/emotional support coach 1x/month - October 2021

7. Had a monitor setup that makes sense - October 2021

8. Had unlimited Breinfuel stock - October 2021

9. Believed that dinosaurs existed - October 2021

10. Met Bryan Hurlman - October 2021

11. Guest spoke for MSU Mankato students - October 2021

12. Did full Wim Hof daily for one month - November 2021

13. Had introspection time daily for one month straight - November 2021

14. Updated my "favorites" list on my phone - November 2021

15. Went ax throwing - November 2021

16. Went to a Tony Robbins conference (UPW) - November 2021

17. Had a success (morning) routine 100 days in a row - November 2021

18. Created a personal mission statement - November 2021

19. Commissioned a personal brand logo - November 2021

20. Thanked a soldier and shook their hand - November 2021

21. Never missed a Funk Thanksgiving - November 2021

22. Got to 200 lbs from bulking - November 2021

23. Benched 260lb again - November 2021

24. Owned a blender bottle for every day of the week - December 2021

25. Hit 10k in podcast minutes in one year - December 2021

26. Nailed a karaoke night at a bar - December 2021

27. Won double Silver Cups with Dane (New biz/total biz) - December 2021

28. Beat Elliot in beer pong - December 2021

29. Saved $10,000 in a year - All year 2021

30. STOPPED "FUNKING IT" (lying about the 'little things') - All year 2021

31. Went to Lambeau Field with my dad - January 2022

32. Went ice fishing with my dad like the old days - January 2022

33. Got to 16 inch biceps - January 2022

34. Was a part of an active Bible study/small group - January 2022

35. Coached someone to a $15k fast start - January 2022

36. Gave a Silver Cup speech - January 2022

37. Got a pedicure - January 2022

38. Did cryotherapy - January 2022

39. Grew a full beard - January 2022

40. Got signed as a model - January 2022

41. Had bloodwork done to find food sensitivity - February 2022

42. Knew all my body's stats (full blood test) - February 2022

43. Went skydiving over an ocean - February 2022

44. Finally fixed the lock on my key fob - February 2022

45. A girlfriend that fully supports and dreams with me - February 2022

46. Hosted Super Bowl with my friend group - February 2022

47. Went to Las Vegas - February 2022

48. Gambled in Vegas - February 2022

49. Met Evan Keller - February 2022

50. Met Bruce Goodman in person - February 2022

51. Rode in a Tesla - February 2022

52. Went to Pawn Stars pawn shop - February 2022

53. Opened a personal alexrfunk.com website - February 2022

54. Went on a Vector national trip - March 2022

55. Maui - March 2022

56. Swam under a waterfall (like in Wild Hogs) - March 2022

57. Touched lava - March 2022

58. Visited the black sand beach/Road to Hana - March 2022

59. Learned how to surf - March 2022

60. Surfed in the ocean - March 2022

61. Went scuba diving - March 2022

62. Met Dan Casetta - March 2022

63. Met Paige Weber - March 2022

64. Met Drew Frank - March 2022

65. Started to learn the piano - March 2022

66. Understood how crypto works - March 2022

67. Updated my YouTube channel to have one artistic theme - March 2022

68. Went to a live rugby game - March 2022

69. Had a YouTube video hit 10,000 views - March 2022

70. Created a LOGO and BRAND for my Vector District office - March 2022

71. Had an article written about me - April 2022

72. Drove a Tesla - April 2022

73. Went to Fogo de Chao - April 2022

74. Went curling - April 2022

75. Thanked 100 soldiers - April 2022

76. Virginia Beach, VA - April 2022

77. Ate at "Cookout" - April 2022

78. Ate at Waffle House - April 2022

79. Bought an iPad - April 2022

80. Went to the NFL draft - April 2022

81. Saw Roger Goodell in person - April 2022

82. Booed for Roger Goodell - April 2022

83. Saw the Eiffel Tower thing in Vegas - April 2022

84. Went to a live magic show - May 2022

85. Opened a District Office with Cutco (DM) - May 2022

86. Officially became a "business owner" - May 2022

87. Earned $2,000 in a week - May 2022

88. Had a staff of 5 in my own business - May 2022

89. Called my mom once per week - May 2022

90. Read daily for three months - June 2022

91. Started a podcast - June 2022

92. Watched a Twins game from behind home plate (with my dad/brother) - June 2022

93. Learned brain dump journaling - July 2022

94. Swam in the Atlantic - July 2022

95. Was told "I'm the best manager ever" 10 times - July 2022

96. My YouTube channel was recognized by Cutco corporate - July 2022

97. Got to only debt that I don't feel bad about - July 2022

98. Had a $5,000 earnings week - August 2022

99. Learned to play one romantic song on the piano - August 2022

***Fifth*** *Dreams Retreat: August 9th, 2022*
*First Dreams Retreat with Ana (138 dreams)*

1. Saw Wicked with Ana (my love) - August 2022

2. Brought 5 people to dreams retreat with me - August 2022

3. Got an AMEX platinum card - August 2022

4. Beat Elliot James at SOMETHING Cutco related (pilot summer CPO) - August 2022

5. Made ginger chicken meal with Ana (her family recipe) - August 2022

6. Took Ana to Valley Fair - August 2022

7. Went to a concert at US Bank Stadium - August 2022

8. Saw Motley Crue with my dad - August 2022

9. Crossed off more dreams every year than the year before - August 2022

10. Owned a week's worth of BYLT shirts - August 2022

11. Always had thank you cards on me (to give to pilots, etc) - August 2022

12. Became an author - August 2022

13. Rode in a convertible - September 2022

14. Cleared out my closet - September 2022

15. Had a man cave station/podcast studio upstairs at our house (The Legendary Dream House) - September 2022

16. Competed in a physique competition (bodybuilding) - September 2022

17. Got back to 8% body fat - September 2022

18. Visited my friend Kendall in Kansas City - September 2022

19. Became a master credit card hacker - September 2022

20. Heard God's voice - September 2022

21. Went on a Cutco factory tour in Olean, NY - September 2022

22. Ate buffalo wings in Buffalo* (if Olean counts...) - September 2022

23. Learned to hook a bowling ball - September 2022

24. Spoke live in front of a Cutco crowd - September 2022

25. Visited Jamestown - September 2022

26. Won the CD3 award (MVP of ChampDev for display of health, wealth, and happiness excellence all at the same time) - October 2022

27. Became an Airbnb Superhost - October 2022

28. Had a $5,000 commission statement - October 2022

29. Bought a meal for someone in line behind me - October 2022

30. Visited my brother again in AZ - October 2022

31. Went to SLC live in person - October 2022

32. Did a pedal pub - October 2022

33. 1099'ed 6 figures in a year - October 2022

34. Bought a giant stack of "one line a day" journals to give away - October 2022

35. Learned about micros not just macros - October 2022

36. Fixed my dead skin on head problem - November 2022

37. Won Vector's Presidents Banquet - November 2022

38. Got a manicure - November 2022

39. Got a coffeemaker at the office - November 2022

40. Went on a road trip that goes through at least 3 states - November 2022

41. Saw Vikings play in Buffalo - November 2022

42. Tailgated a Bills game and crushed a table with Bills Mafia - November 2022

43. Took an overnight train - November 2022

44. Saw Niagara Falls - November 2022

45. Saw a live Broadway show - November 2022

46. Saw Hamilton live - November 2022

47. Rode in an NYC subway - November 2022

48. Saw the Statue of Liberty - November 2022

49. Went on a Europe trip with Ana - November 2022

50. Visited Spain - November 2022

51. Went to Barcelona - November 2022

52. Took a cooking class - November 2022

53. Became a Google expert reviewer - November 2022

54. Rode a Segway - November 2022

55. Ate at a Michelin star restaurant - November 2022

56. Created an ice bath station in our basement - December 2022

57. Coached 10 people to a $6k+ fast start - December 2022

58. Had "meet Alex Funk" on someone else's Dreams List and fulfilled it for them - December 2022

59. Hit $1mil Cutco career sales - All year 2022

60. Finished as #1 overall new DM office in Cutco - All year 2022

61. Fell in love - All year 2022

62. Thanked a soldier every time I saw them - All year 2022

63. Had a success routine every single day of my life - All year 2022

64. Drank a gallon of water every day - All year 2022

65. Journaled every single day of the year - All year 2022

66. Talked to Tess monthly (therapist) - All year 2022

67. Got featured on a podcast - January 2023

68. Got first fully custom tailored suit - January 2023

69. Owned a full baby blue suit - January 2023

70. First nice speaker to play music on - January 2023

71. Painted my office wall black for Zoom - January 2023

72. Volunteered at Eagle Brook Church - January 2023

73. Became incorporated - January 2023

74. Opened Alex Funk Enterprises, LLC - January 2023

75. Took Ana snowmobiling - January 2023

76. Made breakfast in bed for Ana - January 2023

77. Went to the ice castles with Ana - January 2023

78. Visited Baja California - January 2023

79. Got baptized - February 2023

80. Attended Pres. Banq and got the $100 handshake - February 2023

81. Played poker in Vegas - February 2023

82. First full body massage - February 2023

83. Went back and visited my sister in Colorado - February 2023

84. Traveled to London, UK - March 2023

85. Visited Big Ben - March 2023

86. Saw Buckingham Palace - March 2023

87. Explored Westminster Abbey - March 2023

88. Saw a live soccer game - March 2023

89. Watched the changing of the guards - March 2023

90. Crossed London Bridge - March 2023

91. Entered St. Paul's Cathedral - March 2023

92. Rode the London Eye - March 2023

93. Toured a castle - March 2023

94. Saw the Crown Jewels - March 2023

95. Walked across Tower Bridge - March 2023

96. Went to Dublin, Ireland - March 2023

97. Chugged a beer with the Irish - March 2023

98. Visited the Guinness factory - March 2023

99. Explored the Cliffs of Moher - March 2023

100. Toured the Jamison Distillery - March 2023

101. Visited a European art museum - March 2023

102. Finally bought new everyday shoes - March 2023

103. Achieved Google Local Guide status - March 2023

104. Went on a trip with my parents - March 2023

105. Visited sister Kate in CO twice in one year - March 2023

106. Got first paid coaching client - March 2023

107. Broke a Cutco all-time national record - March 2023

108. Saw LeBron James play live in person - April 2023

109. Went to an NBA game - April 2023

110. Got verified on Instagram - April 2023

111. Became more educated on other religions - April 2023

112. Visited Jack Ryan in ATL - April 2023

113. Taught someone how to do affirmations - May 2023

114. Coached a rep to win all-American - May 2023

115. Got a tattoo - May 2023

116. Got a tattoo of Prov 3:5-6 - May 2023

117. Brought in $5k/month consistently from all streams of income - May 2023

118. Watched the movie Pulp Fiction - May 2023

119. Filled a full closet of work shirts - May 2023

120. Flew first class - June 2023

121. Coached 2 reps to win all-American at the same time - June 2023

122. Grilled a steak - June 2023

123. Reached weeks' worth of Lululemon shorts/pants - June 2023

124. Added a 5th bedroom to the 1005 property - June 2023

125. Earned $10,000 in a week - June 2023

126. Bought new workout shoes - June 2023

127. Went to a St. Paul Saints game - June 2023

128. Got a Cutco deluxe hunting knife - June 2023

129. Passed $100k net worth - June 2023

130. Sat front seat on a rollercoaster - July 2023

131. Spoke at SC2 live - July 2023

132. Tipped 100% of the bill - July 2023

133. Drove a jet-ski all by myself - July 2023

134. Reached 1,000 YouTube subscribers - July 2023

135. Had 10 people sitting in Vector's Leadership Academy at one time - July 2023

136. Was featured on 5 podcasts - July 2023

137. Ate at an IHOP - July 2023

138. Got on Vikings season tickets list - July 2023

**Sixth** *Dreams Retreat: August 7th, 2023*
*Ana moved to Minnesota so more dreaming with her*

1. Brought 10 people to dreams retreat with me - August 2023

2. Brought in $10k/month consistently from all streams - August 2023

3. Earned $2k/month in passive income - August 2023

4. Profited six figures in a year - August 2023

5. Got to four streams of income - August 2023

6. Got a sauna - August 2023

7. Got a cold plunge - August 2023

8. Never had dreams limited by money, only time - August 2023

9. Promoted a profitable Branch office within Cutco - August 2023

10. Started my own company (non-Cutco) - August 2023

11. Played disc golf - August 2023

12. Was apart of throwing a surprise birthday party - August 2023

13. Drove a BMW - August 2023

14. Went on a road trip with Ana across the US - August 2023

15. Visited the Rock n Roll Hall of Fame - August 2023

16. Went to Pittsburgh - August 2023

17. Went to Cedar Point in Sandusky, Ohio (world's greatest amusement park) - August 2023

18. Rode the #1 rollercoaster in the world - August 2023

19. Updated pic with the bean - August 2023

20. Ran in-person Cutco training - August 2023

21. Brought back gratitude texts daily - September 2023

22. Went to a legit comedy club - September 2023

23. Took an ice bath once a week for a month - September 2023

24. Went paintballing - September 2023

25. Went to an MN United soccer game - September 2023

26. Positively impacted 1,000 people - October 2023

27. Was a wrap-up speaker at an event - October 2023

28. Went to a trivia night - October 2023

29. Made a perfect steak - October 2023

30. Earned a Rolex in the first full year of being a DM ($1mil office) - October 2023

31. Had a million-dollar Cutco office (yr) - October 2023

32. Got a BMW - October 2023

33. Got a car with auto start - October 2023

34. Had a heated steering wheel in my car - October 2023

35. Visited Houston, TX - October 2023

36. Played pickleball at Hal Elrod's house - October 2023

37. Saw NASA headquarters - October 2023

38. Had my own CLSK episode - October 2023

39. Became a household name in Vector Marketing - October 2023

40. Bought a multifamily property - November 2023

41. Reached 5 doors in rentals - November 2023

42. Helped someone else buy a house - November 2023

43. Visited Puerto Vallarta - November 2023

44. Gave a full paycheck to charity - November 2023

45. Donated $1,000 in a year - November 2023

46. Fully understood the world's biggest religions - November 2023

47. Averaged 8 strain (Whoop fitness band) every day - November 2023

48. Started taking piano lessons - November 2023

49. Made homemade cheesecake (with Ana) - November 2023

50. 1099'ed 200k in a year - November 2023

51. Learned how to play Uno - November 2023

52. Became a Delta status member - November 2023

53. Built a new success routine that includes the Bible - December 2023

54. Learned how to make sushi - December 2023

55. Got a KA-BAR Explorer combat knife - December 2023

56. Started my own coaching business - December 2023

57. Fully believed in the Vector opportunity - December 2023

58. Got offered a brand collab - December 2023

59. Upgraded to an 88 key piano - December 2023

60. Led someone else through a dreams storming session - December 2023

61. Watched the Titanic (movie) - December 2023

62. Baked a cake - December 2023

63. Re-took my food sensitivity blood test to get updated panel - December 2023

64. Was part of a $10 mil Cutco division - December 2023

65. Reached five streams of income - December 2023

66. Crossed off more dreams every year than the year before - All year 2023

67. Get a MN Vikings licence plate - January 2024

68. Go to Orlando, FL - January 2024

69. Disney World - January 2024

70. Run Disney races - January 2024

71. Complete a half marathon - January 2024

72. Get a 2nd phone - January 2024

73. Get an accupuncture - January 2024

74. Buy an Espresso machine - January 2024

75. Two custom tailored suits - January 2024

76. Turn the 'Dream House' into an Airbnb - January 2024

77. Re-do downstairs bathroom at 'Dream House' - January 2024

78. Get a body age test - January 2024

79. Avg 8 strain (Whoop band) every day for a month - February 2024

80. Go to NET (Cutco National Events Training) - February 2024

81. Meet Brandon Brown - February 2024

82. Get cupping therapy done - February 2024

83. Go to Chanhassen Dinner Theater - February 2024

84. Win Vector's President's Banquet every year - February 2024

85. Get a photo with the "Welcome to Las Vegas" sign - February 2024

86. Ride in a helicopter - February 2024

87. Air tour of the grand canyon - February 2024

88. Helicopter over the Las Vegas Strip - February 2024

89. Win a sports bet in vegas - February 2024

90. Get hotel room service - February 2024

91. Eat a sushi burrito - February 2024

92. See the Sphere in Vegas - February 2024

93. The Neon Museum in Vegas - February 2024

94. Ride the High Roller in Vegas - February 2024

95. Drink a gallon of water for 1,000 days straight - March 2024

96. Fully understand organic eating (Watch 'What the Health') - March 2024

97. Go to Madrid (company trip) - March 2024

98. Do a full trip (back) to Barcelona - March 2024

99. Food tour in every country we go to - March 2024

100. Go to Georgia (the country) w/ Ana and meet her fam - March 2024

101. Get engaged - March 2024

102. Destination engagement - March 2024

103. Have my proposal caught on photo by amazing photographer in an unbelievable location - March 2024

And the best is yet to come!

# REFERENCES

## Chapter 1

Buie, D. H. (1981). Empathy: Its nature and limitations. Journal of the American Psychoanalytic Association, 29(2), 281-307.

Thompson, F. (1983). Empathy: an aim and a skill to be developed. Teaching History, 22-26.

Sayce, D. (2023). Social Media Data. https://www.dsayce.com/social-media/tweets-day.

Peng, L., Peng, M., Liao, B., Huang, G., Li, W., & Xie, D. (2018). The advances and challenges of deep learning application in biological big data processing. Current Bioinformatics, 13(4), 352-359.

Crabtree, S. (2005). Engagement keeps the doctor away. Gallup Management Journal, 13(1), 1-12.

Robbins, T. (2011). Notes from a friend: A quick and simple guide to taking charge of your life. Simon and Schuster.

Emotion. (n.d.). https://www.apa.org. https://www.apa.org/pubs/journals/emo.

## Chapter 2

Harvard. (s.s.) https://scholar.harvard.edu/files/danielgilbert/files/if-money-doesnt-make-you-happy.nov-12-20101.pdf

Schiff, S. (2010, December 4). Opinion | Cleopatra's guide to good governance. The New York Times. https://www.nytimes.com/2010/12/05/opinion/05schiff.html

Allen, L. (2006). Being Martha: The Inside Story of Martha Stewart and Her Amazing Life.

## Chapter 3

Theophrastus. (1881). The characters of Theophrastus.

Brown, H. J., Jr. (1991). Life's Little Instruction Book. Thomas Nelson Inc.

Csikszentmihalyi, M. (1997). Flow and the psychology of discovery and invention.

HarperPerennial, New York, 39, 1-16.

## Chapter 4

Nightingale, E. (2019). The strangest secret. Sound Wisdom.

Jones, L., Brett, B., Scott, R. F., & Amundsen, R. (1976). Race to the South Pole. (No Title).

Zigler, zig https://www.centerforperformanceimprovement.com/blog/2017/6/19/how-can-you-hit-a-target-you-do-not-even-have

Matthews, G. (2007). The impact of commitment, accountability, and written goals on goal achievement.

## Chapter 5

Heath, C., & Heath, D. (2017). The power of moments: Why certain experiences have extraordinary impact. Simon and Schuster.

Elle Liu. (n.d.). Forbes. https://www.forbes.com/profile/elle-liu/

Duhigg, C. (2012). The power of habit: Why we do what we do in life and business (Vol. 34, No. 10). Random House

Clear, J. (2018). Atomic habits: An easy & proven way to build good habits & break bad ones. Penguin.

Achor, S. (2010). The happiness advantage: How a positive brain fuels success in work and life. Crown Currency.

Deci, E. L., & Ryan, R. M. (1987). The support of autonomy and the control of behavior. Journal of personality and social psychology, 53(6), 1024.

## Chapter 6

Espegard, Dane. (2021). The Dream Machine

Herrmann, D. (1999). *Helen Keller: A Life*. University of Chicago Press.

*Beyond goal setting to goal flourishing.* (n.d.). https://www.apa.org. https://www.apa.org/pubs/highlights/spotlight/issue-101

## Chapter 7

Huang, S. C. (2023). The Temporal Dynamics of Goal Systems. Goal Systems Theory: Psychological Processes and Applications, 103.

## Chapter 8

Samuel, L. R. (2012). *The American dream: A cultural history*. Syracuse University Press.

## Chapter 9

Espegard, Dane. (2021). The Dream Machine

TOMS. (n.d.). *Blake Mycoskie's Bio | TOMS*. https://www.toms. com/us/corporate/blakes-bio.html

## Chapter 10

Goleman, D. (2017). *Leadership that gets results (Harvard business review classics)*. Harvard Business Press.

Holmes, C., & Heald, A. (2007). *The ultimate sales machine*. Blackstone Audiobooks.

Franklin, B. (1909). *The Autobiography of Benjamin Franklin* (Vol. 41). PF Collier.

Chapter 11

Fiorini, R. A. (2017). An inspired Cultural Revival in Future Education. In *Proceedings of the 2nd International CONGRESS NIKOLA TESLA* (pp. 1-42).

# Chapter 12

Drucker, P. F. (2006). *Classic Drucker: essential wisdom of Peter Drucker from the pages of Harvard Business Review*. Harvard Business Press.

Burchard, B. (2022). *High performance habits: How extraordinary people become that way*. Hay House, Inc.

Hardy, D. (2021). *The Compound Effect (Hindi)*. Manjul Publishing.

Covey, S. R. (1991). *The seven habits of highly effective people*. Provo, UT: Covey Leadership Center.

Roberts, A. (2014). *Napoleon: a life*. Penguin.

# Chapter 13

Nimitz, C. W. (1915). DESCRIPTION OF MAIN PROPELLING MACHINERY FOR THE USS MAUMEE. *Journal of the American Society for Naval Engineers*, *27*(4), 794-821.

Kato, I., & Smalley, A. (2010). *Toyota Kaizen methods: Six steps to improvement*. CRC press

Brown, B. (2022). *The gifts of imperfection: Let go of who you think you're supposed to be and embrace who you are*. Simon and Schuster.

Allen, D. (2015). *Getting things done: The art of stress-free productivity*. Penguin.

Kotter, J. (2012). How the most innovative companies capitalize on today's rapid-fire strategic challenges-and still make their numbers. *Harvard business review*, *90*(11), 43-58.

## Chapter 14

Yttergren, L., & Bolling, H. (Eds.). (2012). *The 1912 Stockholm Olympics: essays on the competitions, the people, the city.* McFarland.

Williams, B. (2015). *Harry Vardon: A Career Record of a Champion Golfer.* Xlibris Corporation.

Nathan, D. A. (2015). "The Nonpareil, the Runner of the Ages": Paavo Nurmi and His 1925 American Exhibition Tour. *Sport History Review*, *46*(1), 154-183.

Hearst, W. R. (1928). *William Randolph Hearst.* Wide World Photos.

Dearborn, M. V. (2004). *Mistress of modernism: The life of Peggy Guggenheim.* HMH.

Inge, M. T. (2012). Li'l Abner, Snuffy, and Friends. *Comics and the US South*, 3-28.

Evans, J. A. S. (1978). What happened to Croesus?. *The Classical Journal*, *74*(1), 34-40.

Parke, H. W. (1946). Polycrates and Delos1. *The Classical Quarterly*, *40*(3-4), 105-108

Made in the USA
Las Vegas, NV
13 September 2024

32376355-5d46-42ac-a1a1-d388665fea87R01